Tim Cole

Wild Wild Web

Tim Cole

WILD WILD WEB

What the history
of the Wild West teaches us
about the future of the
Digital Society

Imprint

ISBN 9781728863757

First edition November 15, 2018

© Forsthaus-Verlag, Forsthausgasse 80, A-5582 St. Michael im Lungau, Tel. +43 (6477) 20253, *forsthausverlag@gmx.at*

Dedication

It was Isaac Newton who once said: "If I have seen further it is by standing on the shoulders of Giants." Two good friends gave me a leg up in writing this book

Gerd Leonhard, Futurist and author of "Technology vs. Humanity", which he (a German) wrote in English and which I (an American) was privileged to translate into German for him, and which inspired me to set out my own thoughts about the future of society in the Age of the Internet.

And I owe an eternal debt of gratitude to Ossi Urchs, the original "Internet Guru"(dreadlocks and all!), with whom I shared endless evenings exploring the digital future for more than 20 years, and with whom I co-authored "Digital Enlightenment Now" shortly before he left us to live on in cyberspace – and in our fondest memories.

Many thanks also to Jean Locicero Shankle and Eric Doyle who shared the arduous task of fact-checking, correcting and improving this book.

Content

Introduction

What the history of the Wild West teaches us about the future of the Digital Society

The short, exciting history of the internet brings to mind the events that shaped the American "Wild West": vast territory was discovered, explored, and eventually, "tamed" (mainly by wiping out the existing native population). Strength and audacity were the only laws and might was right. It took a while, but in the end, the West was parceled out, crops grown and harvested, stage coaches and trains carved inroads, and law was laid down– often at the point of a gun. America sprawled from sea to shining sea, and to this day retains the rough and independent spirit of those who ventured forth without a map.

All this happened much, much faster than most people realize; almost in the blink of an eye, at least in historical terms. The Wild West idealized on the silver screen, in songs and Western novels, took place in a period that lasted about 65 years: that was it!

It all began in 1803. Napoleon Bonaparte was going through one of his periodic cash crunches; fighting the rest of Europe, it seems, cost more than Imperial France could afford. Napoleon decided to sell a few assets, the biggest one being the Mississippi River valley which connected northern French colonies in Canada with southern ones in Louisiana at the mouth of the Mississippi. US-President Thomas Jefferson liked the idea, and between them they clinched the biggest real estate deal in history: 828,000 square miles of unexplored territory for a modest $15 million dollars. Of course, 15 mil wasn't anything to sneeze at back in 1803, working out to around $250 million in today's dollars, but still – what a steal!

Just one year later, the U.S. government decided it wanted to find out what exactly it had purchased, so Jefferson called up two soldiers, Army captain Lewis Meriwether and his friend lieutenant William Clark, who embarked on a legendary 8,000-mile journey of exploration from St. Louis to the Pacific Ocean and back. The 33 members of the expedition and a Newfoundland dog named Seaman trudged for two years across prairies, climbed mountain ranges and forded raging rivers. The Corps of Discovery Expedition, as it was known officially, was sent to document what they observed; they brought back more than 140 maps, descriptions of animals and plant life, as well as news of the Native Americans living in the pristine – as the expedition saw them - wastelands.

By this reckoning, we can count 1804 as the year the legendary Wild West was born. And a mere six decades later, it was all over! On May 10, 1869, the famous "Last Spike" was hammered in at Promontory Summit, Utah, officially completing the transcontinental railroad and opening the continent to travelers, settlers and dealers. The spike, by the way, was forged of solid gold mined in California, and it was effectively the last nail in the coffin of the Wild West. In fact, only three years later, the federal government deemed it necessary to preserve some of the last untouched remnants of the former "Wild" West by setting aside 3,500 square miles of virgin land in parts of Wyoming, Montana, and Idaho, making Yellowstone the world's first national park.

This brief era encapsulates everything we know - or think we know - about the Wild West: gun-toting ruffians, unshaven trappers and tough settlers, stagecoach robberies, the Indian wars and the endless massacre of herds of buffaloes, the service of the Pony Express riders and the stretching of the first telegraph lines.

Less than a century later, in 1962, the greatest film directors of their time, John Ford, Henry Hathaway, George Marshall und Richard Thorpe, joined together to create *How The West Was Won*, a three-hour long Metro-Goldwyn-Mayer epic-western shot in Metrocolor, featuring an all-star cast including John Wayne, Henry Fonda, Gregory Peck, James Stewart and Richard Widmark. It was narrated by Spencer Tracy, who celebrated this short, but special period in the American past, one that had already been embellished, *verkitsched*, glorified and turned into modern myth. Incidentally, this also marked the end of a completely different era, namely the age of epic Hollywood history films.

Will we one day look back on the early decades of the internet in a similar way, as one of mapping the unknown, wrestling for control of vast resources, and cultural prosperity as well as devastation? What will the past tell us about our future?

And we all know what became of the Wild West. The farmers ploughed the land and fenced it in. In 1867, Lucien B. Smith from Ohio received a patent for his invention of barbed wire, which arguably played a greater role in winning the West than the six-shooter. Then came the traders, the surveyors, the shop and saloon owners, the sheriffs, the judges, the bankers, the road and railroad builders turning out the turnpikes and highways. And before we knew it, the land had become "civilized"; law and "order" ruled the land, and in its wake came a type of prosperity, progress, and diversity.

In the Age of the Wild Wild Web, all that still lies ahead of us. Today we are at the same point as the early settlers standing on the shores of the Big Muddy waiting to cross over into uncharted land. For us, this means that the hard work of exploring the cyber-wilderness lies ahead of us. But first, we need to clean things up, create order, pass laws and ensure their enforcement, weed out excess, reign in the bad guys, make the land prosperous and, perhaps this time, more fair for everyone involved.

The big data feast

All this won't be easy, and in fact the prospects aren't that good. The rustlers and cattle (in this case, data) thieves look too powerful. The Googles, Apples, Facebooks and Amazons, whom we will generally refer to in this book collectively as *GAFA*, apparently rule the world. Laws and regulations set up to protect citizens and consumers from their greed appear too puny or simply don't exist. No matter what politicians tell you, the internet is still largely a legal vacuum. Guether Oettinger, Europe's former "digital commissar", was right when I interviewed him 2017 when he called for a European Civil Code; a set of rules that would clarify once and for all who really owns our data.

Oettinger worried about the future of business; if, for instance, no one knows for sure who a CAD file belongs to, which a manufacturer has sent via the Internet to a customer who desperately needs a spare part for his broken-down machine tool. The customer wants to print it in 3D to save time so production gets up and running again, but who produced the part and who, therefore, can claim ownership? Today, nobody knows, and lawyers get to argue the point until the cows come home. Who owns the data my car sends to the car manufacturer every time I visit my local garage? The car makers will tell you its them because you signed over the rights to your data when you accepted their terms and conditions – but did anyone tell you this?

I believe that a decent European Civil Code should not only apply to Europe, but everywhere in the world, and it should set out exactly who my data belong to: me or some tech giant in Silicon Valley?

Huge internet behemoths and tiny startups: they all are accustomed to helping themselves to the information we provide whenever we go online, whether its about our purchasing habits, our most intimate moments, or our secret dreams and desires. And the feast, for them, is free of charge, naturally.

We as society can hardly expect GAFA and their ilk to leave the table without us forcing them to. There's too much at stake, so they will put up a fight. Given their deep pockets and powerful friends in high places, including the 2018 occupant of the White House, for whom regulation and oversight are anathema, the fight may seem hopeless. GAFA has grown accustomed to stealing our data with impunity, to selling the information we provide them free of charge, meanwhile hooking us on their addictive platforms and apps, like drug dealers of the 21st century. And the worst thing is: They don't feel at all guilty! After all, the internet is a free country, isn't it?

And we let them do it.

The Austrian economist Joseph Schumpeter (1883-1950) proposed a theory that he called "creative destruction" in which he describes capitalism as a system that is constantly destroying and recreating itself. On the ruins, innovative companies and new ideas arise – the old ones being relegated to the dustbins of history. According to Schumpeter, demolition is the wellspring of progress and prosperity.

Internet entrepreneurs are constantly providing examples of creative destruction. A key difference between their expeditions into the unknown and the settlers of the old West is that everything is happening at internet speed nowadays. They were IBM and Apple in the 80ies, Microsoft and Netscape in the 90ies, the Big 4 (or Big Five, if you choose to include Microsoft) in the first half of our decade. Today, it's Uber and AirBnB in the West, Alibaba and TenCent in the East: All are out to steal a run off the competition, regardless of the cost for others and for society as a whole.

In 1873, Mark Twain wrote a book entitled *The Gilded Age*, a term he coined to describe the era of the robber barons, specifically John D. Rockefeller, Andrew Carnegie, J.P. Morgan and Cornelius Vanderbilt, to name a few. Between the 19th and 20th centuries, during the years when the West had been "won," gigantic corporate empires were built: powerful monopolies that exploited millions of people virtually unchecked.

Over time, resistance mounted. Workers went on strike and burned down factories. The National Guard was brought in to quell the riots on the behest of the robber barons and their friends, the most powerful politicians of their age.

Will we see similar resistance and unrest aimed at the overwhelming power of the tech giants? Will people take to the streets to demand their rights? Actually, this is already happening as we speak.

On an ice-cold day in February 2012, 16,000 ordinary Germans gathered at the *Siegestor* Monument in Munich to protest against censorship. They carried signs with the message "ACTA ad acta", and their goal was to stop passage of the *Anti-Counterfeiting Trade Agreement* (ACTA), a deal that had been secretly negotiated among the United States, Japan, and the EU.

These "net activists" (what a wonderful word!) were demanding what? The reform of copyright law.

If there ever had been a subject about which I believed the mass of the population cared absolutely nothing about, it would have been copyright law. Well, that just shows you. In Germany, no less, people were standing in the streets demanding their right to copy and share digital content freely. What an awakening! „Wir sind das Online-Volk" ("We are the Online people!"), they chanted, echoing the slogan "Wir sind das Volk" that hastened the downfall of the communist regime in East Germany back in 1989.

On July 4, 2012, the European Parliament voted against ACTA. So you see, it works! The voice of the people will be heard!

And it just keeps getting louder! In June 2015, more than 5,000 taxi drivers took to the streets of Paris to protest against Uber, the ride-share service, whose market capitalization in 2018 lay at $72 bn. The cabbies blocked the roads to airports and train stations. Smoke rose over the Porte Maillot district after irate hacks overturned Uber cars and set them on fire. Policemen were sent to hospital.

The growing opposition to GAFA & Co. doesn't always stem from angry citizens. Administrators the world over are gearing up to put on the thumbscrews. Cities like Berlin and Barcelona have taken to imposing serious fines on home owners who rent to short-term occupants. A number of city governments have forced AirB&B – the world's largest hospitality company – to accept new rules and regulations and to make sure they are enforced. In Berlin, being caught can cost you €100,000 a night! The argument is that affordable housing in Berlin is scarce.

Opinions on this are divided, but by creating a "denunciation portal" where people can report their neighbors if they feel there is too much coming and going next door, authorities in Berlin have definitely overstepped the line. Home owners have taken Berlin to court over their policy which jurists call unconstitutional. Besides, peaching against your neighbors smacks of State Police practiced by the East German communists we just got rid of...

I believe there must be democratic ways of bringing Uber drivers and AirB&B hosts back into legality. This, of course, means that our constitutional state and the rule of law will have to adapt to new realities. What we need are rules that reconcile technology and bureaucracy – no mean task! Cudgeling protesters or fining homeowners is not the answer. What we need today are the willingness and ability to engage in dialog and find creative solutions. If we fail in this, be prepared for more din and tumult. Blockupy was just a foretaste!

What does all this have to do with the Wild West and the robber barons of the Gilded Age? A great deal, I believe. Back in the late 19th century, the reaction against the Big Trusts changed America. In 1902, Theodore Roosevelt became known as the "Trust Buster" when he hauled 45 monopoly owners to court. It was the first time the Sherman Act, an anti-trust law, which had been passed back in 1890, was really applied! From there, history took its course. In 1916, Congress passed the Keating–Owen Act, forbidding child labor. Health and safety regulations were passed.

Historians call the years following the Gilded Age and the breakup of the Big Trusts the Progressive Era. It lasted from the 1890ies up until the Big Depression of the 1920ies. And that is exactly what we need again today: a Progressive Era for the internet!

We need a new, "New [Data] Deal"; one which calls the perpetrators of data theft and sloppy data management to account. Today, since nobody really feels responsible, our data is too often mishandled by companies who let them fall into the hands of criminals, or even cooperate with the bad guys, as the case of Facebook and Cambridge Analytica convincingly proves. But did you ever hear of anyone from Google, Twitter, or Yahoo being fined or imprisoned because they allowed millions of user accounts to be hacked? I haven't either.

In his new book, *Technology vs. Humanity*, my friend, the Futurist Gerd Leonhard calls for the formation of a Global Ethics Council to be charged with drawing up a set of rules and regulations governing how our data are treated and overseeing their compliance. I would go a step further: I believe we need a kind of Global World Inc., a joint-share entity in which we all have a stake and whose job it is to make sure that the profits derived from the sale of personal information are distributed fairly. Think something akin to employee participation. After all, we all work for the big tech companies in one way or another, the internet giants like GAFA, the platform builders and app developers – whether we want to or not. Shouldn't we at least be reimbursed?

Gerd Leonhard also calls for a kind of digital machinery tax, the proceeds of which should go to those who are forced out of their jobs by robots and Artificial Intelligence. Here again, I would go further. Why not divert part of the obscene profits raked up by companies like Apple, which recently posted the best quarterly result in history, into a world-wide relief fund to provide direct assistance to those suffering from the consequences of digitization and automation? Of course, the best idea would be an unconditional basic income for all, but at least for now, that seems to be out of the question politically. But a relief fund could at least lessen the worst effects of advances in technology, and Google and the others should pay for it! They are, after all, the biggest beneficiaries; in fact, they are the only beneficiaries, at least for now.

Perhaps historians will look back on the "Gilded Age of the Internet" and describe it as a hectic time without rules and oversight, in which regulation gradually spread, oftentimes triggered by the industry itself because they finally came around to the notion that it is better to be part of the solution than part of the problem. A time, in which modern robber barons like Steve Jobs, Jeff Bezos, Mark Zuckerberg and Larry Page were able to forge empires, just like their predecessors a century earlier, and who were equally hard to reign in – but who, too, had to submit in the end.

We all seem to believe that the internet has been around forever, but, in reality, we are still at the very beginning. Today the important claims are being staked out in key areas such as video and music streaming, navigation and Cloud services. These are the fields in which GAFA and others will wage wars among themselves, but also against us, the citizens and consumers. The turf is still being marked, and nobody knows who the owners will be.

But one thing is clear: If we just muddle through like before, we will become stuck in the Wild West of the internet. We not only need to demand our rights: we need to fight for them, through the courts, if possible; on the streets, if necessary. To achieve a truly civilized online world, we will need a revolution, and we can only hope that, this time, the revolution will be bloodless.

What we need is a new sense of digital sovereignty. I mean this in a double sense. First, in the legalistic meaning of the term, namely a return of data sovereignty to the digital citizenry. But I also mean it the sense of a certain serenity that comes from the feeling that we have things under control.

As a card-carrying optimist, I believe this is not impossible. I am confident that we will achieve sovereignty and therefore a peaceful transition to a digital era that is based on fairness and order, in every human being has rights to freedom of information, but also to informational self-determination - guaranteed, in which profits are distributed fairly, and performance and rewards are evenly balanced.

Personally, I don't want to live in the Wild West, and if you're honest, gentle reader, you don't want to either. After all, we can always watch it on TV.

Chapter 1: Digital Robber Barons and the second Gilded Age

"We can't blame the technology when we make mistakes."

Tim Berners Lee

John D. Rockefeller   Cornelius Vanderbilt   Andrew Carnegie   J Pierpont Morgan

The „Old" Robber Barons

Steve Jobs   Jeff Bezos   Mark Zuckerberg   Larry Page

The „New" Robber Barons

The first Gilded Age

In 1873, Mark Twain, who most readers associate with children's books like *Huckleberry Finn* or *Tom Sawyer*, wrote a scathing account of American society in his time that he called *The Gilded Age – A Tale of Today*. In it, he described post-Civil War America as "an age of expansion and corruption, of crooked land speculators, ruthless bankers and dishonest politicians".

Twain had personally experienced the old Wild West: Born 1835 in Missouri as Samuel Langhorne Clemens, he spent his boyhood in Hannibal, a small town on the banks of the Mississippi River, which formed the border between the settled East and the "wild" West. He grew up among gamblers, miners, whores and gunslingers, whom he later described brilliantly in his novels and travelogues. He went on to become a river pilot on the "Big Muddy", as the Mississippi was knicknamed, with its many shallows and sand banks. "Mark Twain" was a sounding call meaning that the steamer has a safe 12 feet of water under her keel, and Clemens adopted it as his pen name.

It was a time of blossoming prosperity. The Civil War ended with the fall of the South in 1866; three years later, the first transcontinental railroad connected the two coasts for the first time, making travel across the land mass of the United States much easier. The great white space on early maps of the nation denoting *terra incognita* were rapidly filling up, greatly helped by gold rushes in California (1848), Colorado (1858) and South Dakota (1874) that created huge capital reserves that scrupulous businessmen like John D. Rockefeller, Andrew Carnegie, Cornelius Vanderbilt and John Pierport Morgan used to build market-dominating monopolies in key industries such as steel, oil, railroads and banking.

Simultaneously, the greatest wave of immigration the nation had ever seen set in, with more than ten million foreigners entering the country in search of wealth and opportunity. The "Robber Barons", as they became known, exploited these new arrivals shamelessly. What appeared to be an age of prosperity and progress was, for most Americans, actually a time of poverty and despair, due to rampant corruption and absolute power in the hands of the oligarchs. The "Big Trusts", as they became known, drove prices higher and higher, cut wages at will and called in the police or the National Guard if workers had the temerity to protest or go on strike. Their friends in high places, in city hall or Congress, were more than glad to help them out.

For these greedy capitalists, America at the end of the nineteenth century was the land of limitless opportunities, but for workers and shop clerks, it was not. Finally, the common worker had had enough and began to push back. The movement that started around 1890 and would continue on into the 1920s became known as the "Progressive era", and roughly corresponded to the rise of social democracy in Europe in the early 20th century. Whereas Social Democrats in the Old World widely suffered from state repression, America managed to create what at the time was one of the most modern welfare states in the world. Methodically, presidents hardly anyone remembers today such as Chester Arthur, Grover Cleveland, Benjamin Harrison, William McKinley, and William Taft set about tackling the tough problems one after the other: industrialization, urbanization, immigration, and corruption up to the highest levels. Some of the solutions found back then in areas such as administrative reform, financial supervision and labor legislation are still in place today.

The greatest of them all, however, was Theodore "Teddy" Roosevelt, who was sworn in as the 26th president on September 14, 1901. Voters knew him primarily for his "Rough Rider" escapades during the Spanish-American War of 1898, and, in 1900, McKinley made Roosevelt his running mate. After McKinley died of an assassin's bullet, Roosevelt and his second wife, Edith, moved into the White House.

Ten years before, the U.S. Congress passed the Sherman Act, the first of a slew of anti-trust laws. John Sherman, a Republican Senator from Ohio, justified his bill by warning of an alleged danger of socialists cashing in on the continuing exploitation of normal citizens by the robber barons; Sherman claimed this could lead to revolution. The law was, therefore, popular among conservatives and had been passed unanimously by the House of Representatives.

Roosevelt was the first to take the Sherman Act seriously, which brought him the nickname "Trust Buster": In November 1906, his government laid charges against Rockefeller's seemingly all-powerful monopoly, Standard Oil, and five years later the courts decreed that Standard Oil must be broken up into 34 regional companies.

Rockefeller himself, by the way, became one of the biggest profiteers of the court decision. Betting that the breakup would only lead to a short-term decline in share prices, he invested all he could in shares of the smaller companies, which turned out to be a great idea! Demand for automobiles took off in subsequent years, and, with it, the oil market boomed. Rockefeller is estimated to have earned $200 million through his stock deals – about $6 billion in today's money – making him the world's richest individual of that time, the Bill Gates of his day.

Roosevelt took on one monopoly after the other. His case against J. Pierport Morgan's railroad trust Northern Securities was decided by the Supreme Court by the closest of margins, namely a single vote. Northern Securities was dismantled and became history.

Not that Roosevelt really had anything against trusts per se. "Big", for him, didn't necessarily meant bad. All he called for was a sense of proportion. Greed needed to be combatted. Driven by his own gut feeling, Roosevelt established a school of legal thought that was later codified during the 1911 case against Standard Oil as the "Rule of Reason". The same year, the American Tobacco Company was smashed, and the "rule of common sense" was cited in case after case against dominating corporate interests.

The legal principle lasted a long time. In 1982, it was quoted during the case against "Ma Bell", as the American Telephone & Telegraph Company (AT&T) was then known. AT&T had been founded by Alexander Graham Bell himself and it had grown into a network covering the entire North American continent. The U.S. government started proceedings to break AT&T's monopoly in 1974, but it took eight years to win the case: AT&T itself could maintain its monopoly on long-distance calls but was to be broken up into seven regional phone companies, the so-called "Baby Bells".

The regional companies later began to recombine; Bell Atlantic, for instance, bought NYNEX in 1996 and later merged with Verizon. Others were gobbled back up by AT&T, leading opponents to claim that the judges had failed to apply the Rule of Reason and surreptitiously handed AT&T back its market-dominating position. However that may be, instead of a single monopoly, today America has two powerful rivals in the telephone market, Verizon and Century Link. They have plenty of healthy competition, especially since the rise of smartphones, an area in which AT&T Mobile, Verizon Wireless, Sprint and T-Mobile are vying for customers and market share.

The lessons to be learned here are clear: First, monopolies are unsustainable in the long run. Eventually, politics or public opinion will catch up with them, and the Rule of Reason will apply. Maybe what we need today is a "digital rule of reason".

Secondly, no company is too big to fail. That became clear during the financial crisis of 2008 when Lehman Brothers went down the drain after the U.S. government refused to bail it out. The fourth-largest investment bank in America disappeared along with 25,000 jobs, making it, to this day, the largest business failure in financial history, with an estimated price tag of $50 billion.

Companies like Apple, which became the first company to exceed $1 trillion in market value, and Amazon, which achieved the same feat a few months later, as well as Google's parent company Alphabet ($780 billion) and Facebook, whose market cap dropped to $470 following the Cambridge Analytics fiasco, all have been described as "too big to fail" – an assessment open to doubt.

It doesn't take a rocket scientist to discern who the new generation of robber barons are. The abovementioned Big Four, collectively known as GAFA, have accumulated degrees of power far surpassing those of the monopolists of the Gilded Age in the 19th century. One of them, Larry Page, who founded Google in 1998 together with his Stanford classmate Sergey Brin, is now a billionaire many times over. Under the umbrella of Alphabet, a holding company, Google has gathered a wide range of companies from entirely different industries such as YouTube, Nest, Calico, Google X, Google Capital, and Google Ventures. As chairman of the board and CEO of the parent company, Page exerts more power than anyone else in the world of digital business. Another, Steve Jobs, the legendary founder of Apple who died of cancer in 2011, is probably the most divisive character in recent tech history; he is worshiped as a kind of light figure by some and derided as a brutal power broker by others. Jobs nevertheless succeeded in turning Apple around when he rejoined the company in 1997 and made it into the wealthiest company in the world. In Q1 of 2016, Apple announced the largest quarterly profit in history, namely $18.5 billion. Mark Zuckerberg, founder of Facebook, whose 2.2 billion users make it one of the most powerful sites of the social web, was forced to appear in 2018 before a Congressional panel; Zuckerberg was called to explain his company's role in the Cambridge Analytica scandal about the misuse of personal data in the Trump campaign and policies regarding the use of personal data. Jeff Bezos, the founder of Amazon, appears poised to realize his life's ambition of becoming the most powerful retailer the world has ever seen – both online and offline!

These four have accumulated more power than any business leaders before them, and the companies they represent dominate the digital lives of billions of people all over the globe. Just how this story will play out will be the focus of the rest of this book. After all, our future depends on it.

How the Web was won

Before we go on, though, it first is important to understand how young the World Wide Web is and what motivated its founders when they built it.

The Wild West of the internet began in August 1991 in a cafeteria in Switzerland. Two young scientists at *CERN*, the Conseil Européen pour la Recherche Nucléaire, met there over a cup of *café au lait* to discuss an idea that had occurred to one of them, namely Tim Berners Lee. Lee's idea was about how to improve the communication between the European nuclear research facilities more than 2,500 physicists and technicians.

At the time, teams of scientists were putting the finishing touches to the Large Hadron Collider (LHC), a 17-mile-long underground tunnel studded with dozens of superconducting magnets cooled to an intergalactic temperature of -456° Fahrenheit, at which point electrical resistance is reduced to zero. Dozens of teams from many different branches of science needed to work closely together over months and years, and communication had become a serious bottleneck. It often took ages for information to move from one department to another or even from one room to another.

TBL, as his friends called him, was throwing ideas at his colleague Robert Cailliau, a Belgian from Tongeren, a small town on the border of Holland and Germany. Their solution is called *hypertext*. Normally, a text is read linearly from beginning to end, but in 1939 the Argentine novelist and librarian Jorge Luis Borges suggested a "universal library" of interconnected texts that could make all the works of world literature searchable. Years later, the science-fiction author Isaac Asimov borrowed the idea for his *Foundation Series*, and Doug Adams used it in his "trilogy in four parts", *The Hitchhiker's Guide to the Universe*, where he called it the *Encyclopedia Galactica*.

In fact, the idea of a universal library is even older, going back to the 19th century. The true inventor of the hyperlink was a Belgian named Paul Otlet, and if you have never heard of him, you're not alone. Except for the wardens of an obscure museum in the tiny town on Mons, nobody seems to have the faintest idea he ever existed.

Otlet first came up with the idea of a world-wide
network (he used the French word réseau) in 1895. He
envisioned a system connecting millions of people and
enabling them to search through connected
documents, as well as to send each other news and
other forms of information, thus creating social
networks of the like-minded.

On September 12, 1895, Otlet together with his friend
Henri La Fontaine founded the Office International de
Bibliographie, whose aim was to create a universal
world library that he called the "Mundaneum". He
even managed to persuade the Belgian government,
which nurtured the (ultimately futile) hope of
becoming the headquarters of a League of Nations, to
provide generous funds. Otlet began to collect
information about every book, newspaper article,
pamphlet or poster ever published and recording them
on 5x8 inch index cards. Eventually his collection
consisted of more than 12 million of them, each cross-
indexed through an ingenious notation system he
invented, very much like today more elegant system of
electronic hyperlinks.
In 1834, Otlet wrote a book entitled *Monde* in which
he expanded his vision of a worldwide network of
"mechanical collective brains", that he described as a
kind of electronic telescope. Even earlier he had
speculated that it would one day be possible to store
information and data electronically, thus effectively
anticipating the invention of modern computers.

Tragically, in 1939, the invading Germans
transformed the Mundaneum into a museum for
"degenerate art", and most of Otlet's index cards were
burnt. He died impoverished and broken in 1944. It
wasn't until 1968 that a young student named W.
Boyd Rayward discovered the pitiful remnants of
Otlet's collection in a derelict outbuilding of the
anatomical faculty of the Brussels Free University and
made it his job to create a museum honoring the man
who first imagined a world wide web of information.

Bad predictions

The road to the Digital Society is paved less with good intentions and with bad predictions. Experts and pundits are famous for getting it all wrong, so we should all be very careful whose hype we believe and whose roadmap to the future we follow.

Pablo Picasso (1881-1973) once said of computers that they are "completely useless – all they can do is give answers". Was the famous abstract painter, like the Delphic oracles before him, perhaps hiding a tiny kernel of truth inside his ambiguous augury? Unlikely that Ken Olsen, the founder of Digital Equipment Corporation, was being equally subtle when he expounded that "there is no reason anyone would want a computer in their home." IBM, incidentally, had just released the first PC, kicking off the era of true personal computing. Well, DEC soon sank beneath the waves without a trace, so there!

Thomas Watson, the legendary president of IBM, is often quoted with what would appear to be the grandfather of all bloomers when he said, ""I think there is a world market for maybe five computers." Watson had just returned from a sales tour to show off the company's latest vacuum-tube-powered adding machine that was as big as a house, so the home market for one of those babies would have been extremely limited, indeed.

In hindsight, it's really funny how often savvy entrepreneur Bill Gates got it all wrong and still landed on top as one of the richest men in the world. The founder of Microsoft, a company which owes its success to personal computers (and the operating systems running on them), went on stage at Comdex 1994 and proclaimed: "I see little commercial potential for the internet for the next 10 years!" A year later, in a book he co-authored called *The Road Ahead*, Gates would make one of his most well-known blunders: He wrote that the internet was a novelty that would eventually make way to something much better, and that "today's internet is not the information highway I imagine, although you can think of it as the beginning of the highway." This, by the way, was one year after the World Wide Web had been formally launched.

I was personally involved in one of Billy's famous flubs. When I asked him (in an interview for the German edition of *Scientific American*) back in 1985 what he believed the "next big thing" in computing would be, the then 30-year-old Gates stared me in the face and answered firmly: "voice!" He then went on to describe a world in which computers would understand spoken commands and respond by, for instance, reading out e-mails for us. When I asked him how long it would take for this to happen, he answered evasively: "You see, voice is tricky. It might take another three to five years."

Well, he was only off by about two decades, though his prediction is coming right in the end, with voice bots like Apple's Siri, Amazon's Alexa and Microsoft's own Cortana now speaking up and listening. His successor at the helm of Microsoft, Satya Nadella, himself recently made a daring prediction by stating that "conversations are the new platform", making input devices such as the keyboard or mouse obsolete in just few years from now. Will he come closer than his predecessor?

Less often quoted, but which might possibly prove more relevant to the future of the Digital Society, is a prediction Gates made in 1995. He was asked by a journalist how he thought his company's chances were in the case brought against it by the US Justice Department alleging that Microsoft was using its market-domineering power to force PC makers to bundle Microsoft's own web browser, *Internet Explorer*, with their machines to the exclusion of its biggest competitor, Netscape, and other browsers.

Gates dismissed the question with a terse "This whole anti-trust thing will blow over."

In fact, it didn't. Microsoft lost the first round in 2001, with the presiding judge ordering the company's breakup. This "structural solution" (to use antitrust lingo) was later overturned on appeal, largely because under US law being a monopoly per se isn't illegal, but only after Microsoft agreed to a series of "behavioral remedies" including appointing a panel with full access to the company's source code, records, and systems; it had to essentially hand over its crown jewels by publishing the source code for its Internet Explorer browser. In effect, Microsoft managed to escape full responsibility in America, but European regulators were so disappointed with the US government's backdown that in 2013, the EU Commission levied what was then the largest fine ever announced against a tech company, namely €561 million!

Which just goes to show us (and the internet power players) that, like the rustlers and gunslingers of the Wild Wild West, no one can hope to escape the long arm of the law forever.

The stage coach of the Internet

You don't have to look far to find other interesting parallels between the Wild West and the Wild Web. What, after all, did a cowboy need besides his Colt .45? A horse, of course! And what does the denizen of the Digital Age need: A personal computer, of course – the workhorse of the digital era!

True, looking back, life in the early days of the Digital Era was sort of, well, dull, wasn't it? What could you do with a computer then except type long texts and fill in spreadsheets; but hey, that was all there was to do! And then, in the early 1990s, word passed around that there was something called the "internet" that was really cool! You could send each other "e-mails" and even entire files via a secret process called "FTP". The abbreviation stood for File Transfer Protocol, and that's when things really started moving, sort of like the cowboy saddling his horse and moving out to round up cattle rustlers.

Somehow you first had to get "online", which meant hooking up your computer to a telephone line, which in turn involved attaching an acoustic coupler or, later, a modem, and if you, like me, lacked the technical talent for this, you had to persuade a nerd friend to come over to work his magic on your machine.

A few years went by, and one day a new buzzword started making the rounds: "World Wide Web". As neat as it was, surfing the Web in the earlies involved typing in lots of complicated command lines in UNIX, a programming language which everybody at CERN knew quite well. In addition, the available networks were slow, so the system was soon known as the "World Wide Wait".

That was until the day that another bright undergraduate, Mark Andreessen at the University of Illinois, came up with a tiny program that could display whole web pages including hyperlinks, so all users had to do was click on them, and off we went on the breathtaking ride along the data highway. Andreessen named his program *Mosaic*; shortly after, he got together with the famous computer entrepreneur James H. Clark to establish a company they called *Netscape*.

If the computer is the workhorse of the internet age, Netscape/Mosaic became the stage coach, whisking users from place to place and opening up the wide, wild world of the internet to anybody capable of pushing a computer mouse around. At first, nobody knew where to find fun stuff, so you sometimes landed in some pretty strange places. But it was the serendipity of the Web that fascinated us early users, the luck some people had (and still have) in finding or creating interesting or valuable things by chance.

The so-called graphical user interface, or GUI, was Mark Andreessen's big gift to the world, and one that made him fabulously rich (unlike Tim Berners Lee, who gave us the World Wide Web for free and essentially all he got in return was a knighthood from Queen Elizabeth). But for Bill Gates, who had completely underestimated the power of the internet, Netscape was a slap in the face. He immediately ordered his programmers to develop something similar, because he feared that the web browser – here, he did indeed prove far-sighted – would one day endanger his "cash cow", the Microsoft Office product family of computer tools. Should the network one day become fast and resilient enough, he must have thought, it might be possible to rent a text processor or spreadsheet application over the internet instead of paying Microsoft for a CD.

In his book, *Transformational Products*, my friend Matthias Schrader describes what happened then. "Bill Gates protected his platform by drying up all of Netscape's revenue streams. Microsoft's Internet Explorer was given away free to anyone buying a computer. Gates was taken to court for this, but he managed to weather the storm when the Justice Department chickened out and struck a deal, and in the end, Gates saved his platform by blocking

Netscape's ambition to rule the Web. In the end, though it wasn't the mighty duopoly of the WinTel Alliance that won the Web, but the GAFA quartet: Google, Apple, Facebook, and Amazon. Just how this happened and what it means for the future of the Digital Society will be the subject of out next chapter.

Chapter 2: GAFA and how it sees the world

"Power corrupts; absolute power corrupts absolutely"

Lord Acton

How innovation became a four-letter word

In December 2012, the journalist Alexis Delcambre published an article in the French newspaper *Le Monde* collectively referring to the four largest tech firms, Google, Apple, Facebook and Amazon as *GAFA*. "The term has been used before, but only rarely", he wrote, "and mostly concerning critical topics such as tax avoidance or misuse of personal data." At least in Europe, GAFA had already become a dirty word.

In America, on the other hand, the "Big Four" are usually celebrated as powerhouses of innovation "made in USA". Critical voices from the other side of the Atlantic were usually put down as signs of jealousy. Wouldn't Europeans just love to be able to boast one or two examples of corporations able to match GAFA in terms of innovative power?

Instead, they have companies like Siemens and SAP – nice, but not to be compared with GAFA. To understand why, we need to take a closer look at these tech giants.

Google – the steam engine of the Web

If the completion of the rail link between the East and West Coasts marks the end of the Wild West, the founding of Google is a similar milestone in the development of the Digital Society – only it marled its beginning!

"Google knows everything", the saying goes, which explains why so many people turn to their search engine almost reflexively. According to statcounter, its share of the search market worldwide reached 90.91% in 2018 – slightly less (86.64%) in North America, even higher (91.7%) in Europe, and higher yet in India (97.22%). The staticians at *Smart Insight* estimate that Google answers 1.2 billion queries daily on average! Google does this out of the goodness of its corporate heart and for free! At least that's what they say. Their unofficial motto was "Don't be evil" – at least until May 2018, when it was quietly dropped in the new code of conduct its distributes to its employees.

Google was founded by two Stanford students in 1998, themselves products of Califorina's do-gooder culture, a leftover from the days of Flower Power and Free Love. Apple's Steve Jobs once called the old

Google motto "bullshit!", and that seems to be what those at the helm of Google's new parent company, Alphabet, which was founded in in 2015 as an umbrella for what had become a sprawling company conglomerate with its finger in dozens of high-tech pies, though too. After all, a company that earned 12.6 billion in 2017 can hardly get away for long with styling itself a charitable institution.

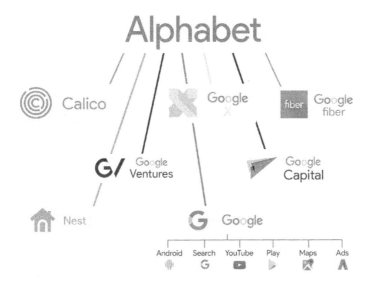

Google's tentacles reach into areas such as biotech (*Calico*), neuroscience (*Google X*), smart heating control (*Nest*), self-driving vehicles (*Waymo*), venture funding (*Google Ventures* and *Google Capital*) as well as artificial intelligence (*DeepMind*). *AlphaGo*, an AI program, was built for the sole purpose of defeating the reigning world champion in Go, the Chinese board game. Readers may ask themselves why go to the trouble? After all, IBM's *Deep Blue* successful challenged the best chess player in the world, Garri Kasparow, as far back as 1996. Yes, but it turns out that Go is about 100,000 times more complicated than chess. "At last, a computer smarter than a human", one headline read when the final match was played in January of 2018.

In reality, it wasn't that fact that a computer beat a human that was significant, but that no human taught the computer how to play the game in the first place. AlphaGo is one of the first instances of what computer scientists call a *self-learning algorithm*. It also taught itself the perfect strategy for beating the world champion, Lee Sedol, a professional Go player from South Korea, without help from any humans. Go experts are still talking about move 37 in the second game of the tournament, where the computer broke with hundreds of years of tradition when it performed a move no human player in his or her right mind would have chosen – and won!

Alphabet may be techs equivalent to a department store, but Google remains its cash cow. Out of Alphabet's $110.9 billion in turnover 2017, Google's main business, called *AdWords*, contributed $95.4 billion.

To grasp the full importance of AdWords, we need to dial back to Google's earliest years when Sergy Brin and Larry Page had the idea to start a search engine that would outperform all the other one already established in the market, of which there were dozens.

In 1993, another group of Stanford students founded *Excite*, which first saw light of day as a research project about Web Crawlers – software robots that creep the web in search for interesting information that they then carry back to their parent servers where they are indexed and offered to users as search results. Excite would go on to partner with Microsoft's own search engine, *MSN*, and with

Netscape, before being sold to the broadband provider @Home.com for $6.7 billion – just as Google was starting to roll up the field from behind. Excite bled market share and was finally forced to file for bankruptcy in 2001. In 2004, the remainders of Excite were bought up for chickenfeed by *Ask Jeeves*, another search aspirant founded in 1997 and going today under the brand name *Ask.com*.

One year after Excite, Yahoo! pioneered a different approach to search by employing human being to double-check the Web Crawler's results. This, unfortunately, cost lots of money, so Yahoo! Tried to persuade companies to pay for being listed in its results, but that also turned out to be a bad idea. The same year, *Lycos*, *Infoseek* and *WebCrawler* entered the fray, followed in 1995 by Altavista and in 1996 by Inktomi. The search market was becoming crowded, but nobody seemed to ba able to figure out a way to turn a profit. The late 1990ies saw a wave of mergers and acquisitions: Altavista and Inktomi disappeared, Yahoo! Was taken over by Verizon, Lycos reinvented itself as an e-mail service provider cum entertainment portal, and MSN was renamed *Windows Live* and in 2009 became *Bing*.

Google may dominate the search market almost everywhere, but one notable exception remains: China! One reason is state censorship, often euphemistically referred to as the "Great Firewall of China", but another is strong competition. The Chinese, it appears, prefer to search local. Baidu, a name meaning "a hundred times" or "countless times" and derived from the last line of the classical eleventh-century poem "Green Jade Table in The Lantern Festival", is kept on a tight leash by the government and makes sure that users don't get to see "undesirable content" such as Western news criticizing Chinese policies. The organization *Reporters Without Borders* accuses Baidu of systematically removing "subversive" content from its search result.

In protest, Google withdrew from Communist China in 2010, but apparently the stakes are too high for Google's new parent company, Alphabet, to completely ignore. The company recently opened two new offices in Beijing and Shanghai, a third is scheduled to open soon in Shenzhen. Plans are also underway for a new research facility in Beijing which will concentrate on artificial intelligence (AI) – an area where China has announced its goal of becoming a world leader. Of course, the real reason Google is returning to China isn't love of knowledge, but the wish to tap China's vast pool of highly skilled software engineers. Insiders are sure that Google's tightening embrace of Chinas dictators will one day lead to the company reneging on promises and quietly opening a – censored – version of its search engine in Mandarin.

After all, its all about business. Google was the first player to discover how to make money – lots of money – with search. While others vainly struggled to introduce business models such as "paid search", in effect forcing enterprises to pay up every time a user clicked on their name, Brin and Page had the bright idea to concentrate on "relevant" advertising. Their brainchild, AdWords, enabled companies to book certain key words and only pay once users have actively searched for them. Since the number of ad spaces is limited, this forced advertisers into a bidding war in which they themselves determine how much they are willing to shell out in someone clicks on their ad. This can range from a few cents for fast-moving items like consumer goods to serious sums for high-end goods or services. The most expensive AdWord, according to SearchMetrics, a specialist in what is known as "search engine optimizing" (SEO), was *outplacement*, for which advertisers were willing to pay almost $70 a pop! Outplacement, it seems, is a profitable business, offering employers a cheap way of getting rid of surplus personnel.

"This ingenious mechanism creates an invisible bond between the user's intention and matching advertisements", says Matthias Schrader, the founder of *Sinner+Schrader*, a German online advertisement agency that was recently aquired by Accenture. In his book, *Transformational Products*, Schrader explains how Google's AdWords system ensures that Google always gets the best deal. "The user reveals what he or she really wants by typing in a keyword. Google's algorithms pick the ad that most closely fits the user's desire and sells the user's attention to the highest bidder, an that in real-time. And the advertiser is happy because it was he who agreed to pay the price in the first place."

AT first, advertisers were skeptical, and the average price-per-click was a few cents. But the system had obvious benefits, not the least the fact that it provided a simple and convincing metric for gauging an ad's success. Besides, it gave advertisers a way to test different versions of an ad against each other, so that they could restrict themselves to AdWords with a proven *conversion rate*; a customer who purchase something at the webshop is be considered to be "converted". And even those who only look at the ad and move on are known at least to be potential buyers and can be contacted again and again in the future.

Over the years, two separate industries have sprung up around the subject of conversion. One, *search engine optimization*, or SEO, involves painstaking testing to determine how even minimal changes to an ad can influence the willingness of users to take the plunge and become buyers. The other, *search engine marketing*, or SEM, namely the fine art of increasing an ad's visibility. Both employ thousands of "search professionals", each dedicated to improving an advertiser's *page ranking* and thus his or her conversion rate. Automation plays a huge role in both disciplines, and hundreds of specialist agencies that have become indispensable to almost any company interested in boosting its online business. Alternatively, large companies often prefer to establish their own departments, but good SEO and SEM people are hard to find.

However, there are increasing signs that Google has already pushed its business model to its limits. Bid wars for AdWords that convert well have driven prices to often ruinous levels, meaning that vendors struggle to reach their bottom lines. Matthias Schrader compares this to game theory, where the *prisoner's dilemma* is a well-known phenomenon: "In order to gain market share at the cost of their competitors, companies are forced to reduce their profitability by paying more and more for good AdWords. If, on the other hand, they opt to increase their margins, they lose market share and sales volume", he says.

Any way you look at it, only one wins in the end – namely Google!

Dirty game?

Besides, there is a growing suspicion among advertisers that Google is dealing from the bottom of the deck. Other search engine operators have accused Google of manipulating their algorithms to make sure certain pages don't appear among the top-ranking search results and hence don't convert well. There have been instances of Google forcing advertisers to agree not to promote ads from its competitors. *Foundem*, a British price comparison engine, and *ejustice.fr*, a legal data base, have both filed suit against Google for allegedly locking them out of its search results. In 2010, Microsoft, which operates a recommendation portal called *Ciao*, filed cartel proceedings against Google with the European Commission in Brussels, alleging that Google was abusing its dominant position in the search market to harm consumers and competitors. In June 2017, the European Union fined Google $2.6 billion, the second-highest financial penalty in its history. Should Google refuse to comply, the Europeans pronounced, it could be fined up to five percent of its average global daily turnover, about $16.5 billion. Even an Internet giant would feel the pain.

In America, Google got off more lightly. Before the Federal Trade Commission (FTC), Google successfully argued in 2011 that its habit of discriminating against the competition was covered by its right to free speech. Given the importance the First Amendment enjoys in the U.S., the watchdog agency withdrew its complain in 2013, but not before confirming that Google did, indeed, prioritize its own search results.

Another frequent complaint against Google is that the search engine behemoth treats its customer's data as its own, to be stored, repackaged and sold to any interested buyer. Google's long-time CEO Eric Schmidt, despite his German-sounding name a true-born American, told the *Wall Street Journal* in 2010 that Google is out to gather as much information about its users as possible. "I actually think most people don't want Google to answer their questions; they want Google to tell them what they should be doing next", he was quoted as saying. For this, in 2013 Google received the Big Brother Award from the German Chaos Computer Club (CCC), a human rights organization, which it bestows annually on a company known to interfere most brazenly in its user's privacy. Constance Kurz, the spokeswoman of CCC, told the radio station 3sat: "Google is less a search engine operator and more an aggregator of personal data." And Peter Schaar, the German Federal Privacy Commissioner, recently complained that "Google provides a search screen whose main purpose is to collect user information which allows it to compile a very precise picture of what I am interested in and how I behave."

If Google, as stated at the beginning of this chapter, can be best compared with the railroad giants of the Wild West, then the solution is obvious. The "Railroad Tycoons" of the late 19th century such as George Gould, Cornelius Vanderbildt, Edward Harriman and Collis P. Huntington, also referred to than, funnily enough, as the "Big Four", fought each other bitterly for the hegemony of the railroad networks, which had grown between 1840 and 1916 from a total length of 2.800 miles to an astonishing 250.000 miles. Competing railway lines were often built next to each other, with teams of workers occasionally exchanging shots at each other. The railroad barons staunchly refused to introduce safety measures, arguing that they would cut into their profit margins. Farmers in the Midwest were forced to pay outrageous rates to transport their crops to the markets of the East. In 1887, Congress finally became fed up and passed the *Interstate Commerce Act* which put the railroads under supervision and forced them to publish their rates, effectively ending their habit of charging greatly inflated rates for farmers in the remoter regions of the West. As a result, the tycoons began to consolidate their companies into large regional or national lines that were able to survive into the 1930ies, when the Great Depression and the rise of the automobile put an end to most of them. Today, the rail networks still stretch almost as far as they did at the turn of the century, but they are now mainly used to transport goods; modern-day passengers in America continue to ride only about 22.000 miles of rails. Cars and planes have had a similar disruptive effect to that of digital technology today.

So what does this say about the future of Google? That is something we will discuss further in chapter 3.

Amazon – the jack of all online trades

Somehow the idea persists among many people that Amazon invented e-commerce. In fact, Amazon is only responsible for about half of all online sales, but only three quarters of this admittedly are a direct part of Amazon's core business. The rest, about 25%, is handled by Amazon Marketplace, where third-party vendors are invited to conduct their business, for which Amazon charges them a fee of about 25% off of every article sold.

To find a parallel between Amazon and the Wild West, one has to only look back as far as 1886. That was the year a railroad agent named Richard Warren Sears bought a crate full of watches that had been delivered to his station in North Redwood (MN) but never picked up. He placed ads in various newspapers throughout the Midwest, and his tiny firm which he named *R.W. Sears Watch Company* quickly managed to sell its entire stock at a substantial profit. A year later he made the acquaintance of a watchmaker called Alvah Roebuck who knew how to repair watches, and the two went into business together.

Sears printed his first mail-order catalog the same year, in which he offered not only watches, but also diamonds and jewelry. In 1889, the two partners relocated to Chicago and founded a new company, *Sears, Roebuck & Company*. A legend was born.

The Wild West was, admittedly, a little tamer by then: thousands of farmers had settled the Great Plains who often had to travel great distances to reach the nearest General Store where choice was limited and prices high.

Sears Roebuck, on the other hand, were comparatively cheap, their range broad. Business boomed, and the two kept adding new items to their increasingly hefty catalog which had grown to 532 pages by 1895. You could buy almost everything by mail order; dolls and sewing machines, bicycles and sporting goods, later even automobiles manufactured for Sears by the Lincoln Motor Car Works in Chicago. In 1896, kitchen stoves and dry goods were added.

In 1893, the United States went through a stock market crash that led to a severe depression, and Alvah Roebuck was caught short, so he sold his shares for $75.000 (or $2.2 million in today's money) to Julius Rosenwald from Illinois, an experienced businessman and manager. Rosenwald introduced modern management methods and expanded the product line. In 1906, he took the company public and gathered in $40 million ($1.1 bn at today's dollar valuation) from investors, which he used some of the money to build the 14-storey Sears Tower in Chicago, the highest building in the Windy City at that time.

Many years later, in 1973, the successor to the old Sears Tower became the tallest building in the world, and it remains Chicago's landmark to this day, even though Sears was forced to move out in 1995 and the skyscraper was sold to a London insurance company called Willis Group who unsuccessfully tried to rename it. For native Chicagoans, thought, it remains Sears' Tower to this day.

Real estate was the ruin of Sears Roebuck. Its mail-order business focused on rural customer, who however were increasingly becoming wealthy enough to afford cars. Starting in the 1920ies and continuing up until the 1950ies, Sears embarked on a building spree, erecting big department stores in almost every mall that sprang up in the suburbs of the big urban metropolises. At their height, Sears Roebuck owned thousands of stores across the nation, and in 1993 the wrenching decision was reached to discontinue publishing the company's hallmark catalog with which it all began. Unfortunately, the department store business started to go into decline during the 90ies. Kmart took over the ailing business in 2004 and reduced the number of stores, which dropped from 3,500 in 2010 to 695. By April 2018, there were only 555 stores left, and financial analysts believe that Sears/Kmart will eventually disappear from the market altogether.

Fast-forward to 1993, when Jeff Bezos was driving from New York to Seattle, and somewhere along the way he had this bright idea. Legend would have it that Bezos never intended to become the world's biggest bookseller – that would have been too small a dream for an ambitious guy like him. From the very beginning, Bezos really wanted to become the world's biggest retailer – nothing less! Books just happened to be an easy starting point.

His dream, it seems, is rapidly coming true today. One important milestone was reached in March 2018, when Bezos overtook Bill Gates in *Forbes'* list of the world's richest people. At the time his fortune was estimated to be worth $110 billion!

Like all good startups, Amazon first saw the light of day in Bezos' garage. The idea for the name came to him because he always wanted to go on an expedition to the Amazon. Besides, if he ever founded a company, he always said its name would have to start with an "A" so it would rank way up there on the search results. His parents lent him $300.000 they had originally earmarked for their retirement savings. He admitted to them and other early investors that there was about a 70% chance he would be unable to pay them back since his firm might not survive through its first year.

Well, Amazon made the cut, and in 1998 Bezos added music and video CDs to his lineup, followed a year later by a wide range of consumer goods. He took Amazon public and stuck every cent of the $54 million he earned back into the company, buying up lesser competitors left and right and starting an online service he called Amazon Web Services (AWS), that collected and sold weather and traffic data. Not every acquisition panned out, and in 2002 Amazon was almost bankrupt. Instead of folding, Bezos persuaded his bankers to lend him a staggering two billion dollars, closed a couple of unprofitable ventures and send 14 percent of his workers home. A year later, Amazon was back in the black, earning $400 million before taxes.

In November 2007, Bezos launched the Amazon Kindle, an e-book reader. Not that there was any appreciable market for e-books at the time, but Bezos believed their time had come. Analyst dismissed him and foretold his quick demise: "This time, Bezos has gone too far!"

Instead, Bezos' crazy plan actually worked! People began to engage and interact with books the same way they had been doing with Videogames for years. Sales of e-books skyrocketed, and Bezos' Kindle took off, too. By 2017, more electronic books were being sold in America than paper ones.

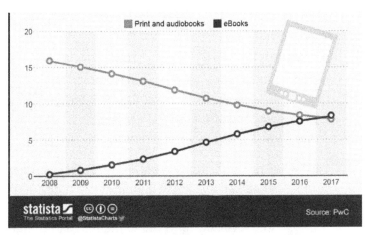

Since its foundation, Amazon has been at the center of an acrimonious debate about whether it wil be the death of old-fashioned bookstores or not. Time will tell, but the signs aren't all bad: In Germany, for instance, book sales dropped only insignificantly between 2011 and 2017, namely from €9.8 bn to €9.05 bn. In America, book sales were even up 1.9% in 2017 according to *Publishers Weekly*. And Amazon itself has begun a chain of bricks&mortar bookstores in selected inner-city locations in North America, so maybe there is still life in the old business model.

However, Amazon's outlets are quite unlike the old mom & pop bookstores. For one thing, they sell more than books; at least a quarter of the shopfloor at Amazon's Manhattan flagship store is reserved for things like electronic gadgets, Bose loudspeakers, disc drives, digital cameras and of course Amazon's own Kindle readers.

"Amazon bookstores don't do much business", an article in the trade magazine Business Insider stated in 2017, "but they are an important building block in Amazon's overall strategy which is all about Jeff Bezos's brilliant idea called *Amazon Prime*."

Prime Time

Prime is much more than just a classic customer retention scheme. As Matthias Schrader writes, "Prime was one of Amazon's very first transformational products – for three reasons:

- First, Prime ups the ante in terms of customer expectations. Prime members can order anything in the world that carries a barcode, and it will be delivered to them free of charge and faster than anywhere else. Amazon has invested great sums in its logistics and delivery services, and they're miles ahead of the competition as a result. Due to *Same-Day Delivery,* shopping at Amazon is actually faster and more convenient than driving to the mall, at least if you live in an urban area.
- Secondly, Amazon has expanded the Prime experience into other areas such as *Prime Music, Prime Video, Prime Photos,* an online lending library (*Prime Reading*), as well as a gaming and merchandise portal (*Twitch Prime*). In effect, Amazon has created a huge customer loyalty platform which binds consumers to Amazon voluntarily. All of this is included in the price of a Prime

membership which was raised in May 2018 from $99 to $110 without denting the program's popularity. Schrader quotes market research from *Millward Brown Digital* claiming that the probability of a Prime customer actually purchasing something is a whopping 74 percent – 20 times the rate of a normal webshop!

- And thirdly, says Schrader, Amazon isn't a real merchant at all but instead an errand service. "Bezos isn't interested in building the best tablet or e-reader. For him, atoms are just the necessary physical embodiment of a service." Amazon is so successful in E-Commerce, he believes, because it doesn't play by the rules other vendors follow.

Amazon has transformed commerce – and not just the online variety, either – almost beyond recognition. Not everyone is happy about this. The company is under pressure from various directions. In 2015, the *New York Times* published an article detailing the scandalous conditions warehouse employees at Amazon were forced to work under, often laboring for 55 hours a week under forced overtime, which led to frequent cases of staff collapsing on the job and requiring emergency medical attention. Toilette breaks were limited. In the UK, temporary workers were required to report on the job seven days a week and were fired if they called in sick, the *Times* wrote.

Opening another front against Amazon, Donald Trump complained (via Twitter, of course) that the retailer was ripping off the U.S. Postal Service, using its market power to extort price cuts for package deliveries, ostensibly causing billions in losses for the postal service. As usual when Trump butts in, a heated debate ensued in early 2018 about the truth of the President's allegations, along the lines of "Is Amazon the savior or the destroyer of the postal system?"

As if all this wasn't enough, Amazon is under siege from all over the world because of the way it dodges tax local laws on both sides of the Atlantic. In the U.S., Amazon paid virtually nothing in 2017, despite reporting roughly three billion dollars before tax earnings. This was only possible by exploiting just about every legal loophole they could find, such as massive write-downs on investments in R&D and manager bonuses. Amazon has also been very successful in avoiding having to pay sales tax, although it must be said in all fairness that this practice was sanctioned by the Supreme Court in 2017. American online retailers in general enjoy an unfair advantage over their bricks&mortar competitors. Unless they were physically located in the same state as a shopper, they were not obliged to collect state and local sales taxes. In theory, shoppers were legally required to pay sales taxes on stuff they purchased online, but nobody did. Since state and local sales taxes can add up to as much as 12% of a product's price, this gave online dealers, especially Amazon, a huge advantage. But on June 21st, 2018, the Supreme Court reversed itself and ruled that online retailers did have to collect sales tax themselves.

Amazon has argued for years that it is only subject to the tax laws in places where they operate a physical presence, which essentially meant that they only paid taxes in their home state, Washington. However, over the past years Amazon has erected giant distribution facilities all over the United Stated and the rest of the world, each one effectively establishing a physical presence and thus obliging the company to ante up. It has been reluctant to do so, and it now is facing proceedings brought by tax authorities in Germany, France, the UK, and Luxembourg. In 2009, Japan forced Amazon to accept a bill for ¥14 bn (about $119 mil) in back taxes.

While it might seem as though Amazon is up against a wall, facing their obligations as a taxpayer may prove a boon in the long run. After all, the ruling applies to the competition, too, so any cheeky startup trying to undercut Amazon through the old loopholes will be in trouble. Besides, it will stop many consumers from effectively using Amazon as a search engine for checking prices before moving on to other retailers who may offer the same product a few cents cheaper. The *Economist* wrote recently: "Amazon, which once lobbied against legislation requiring online retailers to charge sales tax, has in recent years switched to lobbying in favor of them."

Seen together, these various strands of criticism may seem par for the course for a company as large and successful as Amazon. However, trouble is brewing on another front, far away from the glare of the public spotlight. This touches a more general question, one which pertains to the other members of GAFA, too, namely do we need to reconsider our entire system of addressing competition and fair trade in the era of the World Wide Web? Or, to put it another way, are our Antitrust Laws hopelessly out of date?

Market-driven censorship

Everybody know what a monopoly is. But what is a monopson? A monopoly is where many buyers face a single seller, the classic example being the U.S. Postal Service back in the days when it was the only company licensed to deliver letters and packages, so it could set its prices ad libitum, with only the United States government in a position to reign them in through oversight.

A monopson works the other way around. The word comes from the Greek *mono* (for "single") and the verb *opsōnia* (for purchase of food) and is defined by the *Free Dictionary* as "a market situation in which the product or service of several sellers is sought by only one buyer." The classic example here could be the U.S. military, which in effect represents a single buyer who purchases from numerous competing members of the industrial-military complex.

Paul Krugman, the Nobel Prize-winning economist and columnist for the *New York Times*, wrote back in 2014 that Amazon "has too much power", and that it abuses its power systematically. To understand this we need to know that Hachette, on of the biggest publishing houses in France, and Bonnier, the Swedish media conglomerate, were locked at the time in a bitter fight about eBooks on Amazon. Amazon wanted a bigger slice of the cake, which the publishers were unwilling to grant. To force the intransient booksellers into submission, Amazon simply tweaked their algorithms until eBooks from Hachette and Bonnier began landing at the bottom of the heap. As a result, sales of bestseller authors like Ingrid Noll (*The Pharmacist*), Gunter Wallraff (*Lowest of the Low*) and Nobel Prize-winner Elfriede Jelinek (*The Piano Teacher*) plummeted.

Apparently adding insult to injury, Amazon began taking longer and longer to deliver books from the effected publishers who eventually called Jeff Bezos out in an open letter, accusing him of holding them and their authors hostage and thus working against the interests of their readers. "Amazon thereby directly contradicts its own pledge to be 'the earth's most customer-centric company'", they wrote.

Amazon is prime example of the kind of unbridled power the era of GAFA has allowed digital operators to accumulate and exercise. In the case of Amazon versus the publishers, one might well ask: so what? Who cares if one filthy-rich corporation applies the thumbscrews to another filthy-rich corporation who happens to be its supplier? It's a free market, ain't it? That's just business as usual.

Not so, argues Paul Krugman. What would stop an unbridled Amazon from suppressing content it deems politically incorrect? Could free markets lead to censorship? Why not, he asks, and raises a warning flag. Amazon's behavior, he believes, isn't just evil and unethical in itself; it's also bad for trade and markets. Unfortunately, Krugman complains, our anti-trust laws are hopelessly out of date and completely unable to act against monopsons. This must change, he demands.

Facebook – the teetering giant

Whether Facebook is a blessing or a curse for society is a matter of hot debate. One thing is clear, however: It brings people together. Were Facebook a nation state, it's population of about two billion active users would surpass both China and India.

To judge the true significance of the company founded in 2004 by Mark Zuckerberg, a computer science dropout from Cambridge University, we need to make a whole slew of comparisons, for instance the first transcontinental railroad in the U.S., the Pony Express riders, or the invention of the telegraph.

The Wild West was a lonesome place: settlers lived way out in the boondocks, far from the nearest church or general store where people tended to meet and gossip. At the time of the California Gold Rush auf 1848, delivering a letter from New York to San Francisco around Cape Horn took about 90 days.

Yet another date marking the passing of the Wild West was January 27, 2006 – the day Western Union sent its last telegram over the wires. For 145 years, those thin strands of copper had provided the only unbroken connection between East and West Coast.

The telegraph changed America forever. The country began to shrink and close ranks. Suddenly, news could travel from one end of the continent to the other in a matter of hours. The man who created this communications revolution was a gifted tinkerer named Samuel Morse. A portrait painter by profession, Morse earned enough to put himself through university with his miniature likenesses which he customarily sold for five dollars apiece. In 1811, he was asked to become a member of the Royal Academy in London, so good were his portrayals. Nothing at the time indicated that he would go on one day to make it big in telecommunications.

In his spare time, Morse experimented around with primitive batteries and magnets. He assembled his very first working telegraph, appropriately for a painter, on an easel. In a frame, he installed a pencil attached to an electric powered pendulum and was able to draw lines and dots of a moving strip of paper every time the current was switched on. He went on to develop the alphabet of dots and dashes that still bears his name, "Morse Code", and with which it was possible to send messages over connecting lines. On May 24, 1844, Morse sent the world's first telegram from Washington to Baltimore, a distance of about 160 miles. He borrowed his text ("What Hath God Wrought!") from the Book of Numbers.

In 2007, Daniel Walker Howe published a book called *What Hath God Wrought – the Transformation of America*, which earned him a Pulitzer Prize. For us living in the age of Digital Transformation, the title rings a bell.

The second stage of the nascent upheaval in communications was lit in 1876 when Alexander Graham Bell, a Scots-born deaf-mute teacher, applied for a patent for an invention he called the "acoustic telegraph". In fact, Bell had a working model of a machine built by the German inventor Johann Philip Reis standing on his workbench when he completed his application. Reis, a physics teacher, had named his invention the "telephone".

Bell wasn't just good at copying the ideas of others; he was also faster then they were. The very same day Bell handed in his patent application, Elisha Gray, a blacksmith from Ohio who was working as an instructor at Oberlin College, submitted his own patent. He was four hours late. American courts would go on to deny over 600 lawsuits against Bell's patent, but in the meantime he has managed to found a company that created a virtual monopoly in North America. The *Bell Telephone Company* was renamed the *American Telephone & Telegraph Company* (AT&T) in 1855 and would go on to become the biggest network operator in the world.

Bell changes America even more drastically than Morse had done. From his New York headquarters, Bell's twisted cables began to spread their web all over the country and, eventually, the globe. In 1892, the telephone reached Chicago, by 1915 calls could be made to San Francisco. Soon, every farmer in the Midwest had a handset hanging on the wall and could talk to anyone else in the remotest corners of America. The price to be paid in the early days was that your neighbors could usually listen in on your calls. Telephone lines were expensive, so most households in the West shared what was known as a "party line". You knew if someone was listening in by the distinctive click if someone picked up their phone, and generations of young lovers grew accustomed to asking the neighbors to please hang up before whispering sweet nothings into each other's ears over the receiver.

In 1913, the U.S. government became convinced by the argument out forward by Theodore Vail, the CEO of AT&T, and granted his company a monopoly on all long-distance calls in America. A monopoly, Vail maintained, was more efficient that the hodgepodge of small regional carriers who had sprung up over the preceding decades. In fact, AT&T already had a firm hand on the regional markets around the country through an interlocking system of22 so-called *Bell Operating Companies*, often fondly referred to as *Baby Bells*. In 1974, the government performed an about-face and ordered AT&T to be broken up into independent regional operators. AT&T, however, was allowed to keep its long-distance monopoly.

Today, thanks to a series of takeovers and mergers, AT&T is back in business as never before. In 2016, it acquired Time Warner. An attempt to purchase T-Mobile USA from Deutsche Telekom for $39 bn was foiled in 2011 by the Federal Trade Commission.

Telegraph and telephone have changed the world in ways very similar to today's Social Web. Distance and location have become increasingly irrelevant both in our private and our business lives. They have changed the way we communicate and enriched our everyday lives immeasurably.

Good isn't good enough

We ceased to send each other telegrams years ago; instead, we're constantly on the phone.

The same thing happened 100 year later: A good thing, namely *MySpace*, was swept away by something better – *Facebook*! MSpace was founded in 2003, long before the current reigning champ of the Social Web, but today it's a forgotten backwater on the sleazy side of the web. In 2004, MySpace boasted a million users per month and seemed on its way to the very top. In 2005, Robert Murdoch's *NewsCorp* acquired MySpace for a staggering $580 m and announced its goal of reaching 200 million users and a stock valuation of $9 bn.

But then, suddenly, MySpace seemed to run out of steam. In March 2009, flush with cash from the buyout, key executives began to leave the company in droves to found their own start-ups. In April, CEO and co-founder Chris DeWolfe followed suit, and in June MySpace was forced to let go of a third of their staff. A second round of firing followed in January 2011, culling a further 50 percent of the workforce.

What had happened? For one, Facebook had begun to take off after a slow start, and by June 2008 had overtaken MySpace in the number of active users. One year earlier, MySpace had made international headlines as the "favorite meeting place for paedophiles". The company barred more than 90,000 sex offenders from using its services, but the damage was already done.

The real problem, though, stemmed from the takeover by NewsCorp. In a speech at the Oslo conference *By:Larm* in 2015, Sean Percival, who headed the marketing department from 2009 to 2011, gave an insider's view of what went wrong at MySpace. "The reality was that as time went on, the corporate policies creeped in", he said. "The lawyers came in, the accountants; everything came in. As opposed to this nimble, fast-moving sports car, they started to become slow." Besides, the Department of Justice was coming after MySpace because of all the kiddie porn and sex trafficking. "There was truly weird stuff going on on MySpace", he admitted, "but MySpace said 'hey, we don't care! We're from Los Angeles, sex is what drives the economy out here. We're happy to have you. So bring in Tila Tequila'."

Today, hardly anything remains from the glory years of MySpace. From a peak of 76 million users have declined to maybe 15 million. Murdoch, who eventually admitted that buying MySpace was "a big mistake", sold the portal for a piddling $35 million to the ad network Specific Media, and in February 2008, Elise Moreau of *Lifewire* asked: "Is MySpace dead?"

Why should we study the sad case of MySpace? Because it shows how transient even huge digital behemoths like GAFA can be. One major mistake, one false turn, and you're history, buddy!

Facebook was conceived as the online version of the yearbooks popular among American students. Legend has it that Zuckerberg thought this would be a great way to get to know girls on campus. Originally the service was restricted to a handful of colleges and university, but it soon shook off its ties to academia and began to grow exponentially.

Until recently, Mark Zuckerberg seemed to be the man, and there was even talk in late 2017 of his making a bid for the White House in 2020. But then came the Cambridge Analytica scandal during which it was shown that Facebook had at least looked the other way when the company, which worked for the Trump campaign, harvested the personal data of millions of Facebook profiles without the users' consent in order to influence the election. Initially, Facebook refused to comment on the claims, which just made matters worse, especially since complaints about *fake news* – manipulated or falsified allegations launched by various political groups through Facebook accounts registered in false names – became rampant. In May 2018, it turned out that fundamentalist anti-abortionist in the United States were flooding Facebook in Ireland ahead of the referendum that would eventually lead to the rescinding of that Catholic country's ban on abortion. In a headline, *The Economist* called Facebook an "antisocial network".

Dark clouds are hanging over Facebook's headquarters in Menlo Park, and nobody knows if this is just a short-lived PR disaster or the beginning of the end. One thing, however, is clear: The big times are over for Facebook, at least for now. According to a study from the Pew Research Center, record numbers of teenagers are abandoning Facebook in favor of other social media platforms such as Snapchat and Instagram. When asked which of the online platforms teens used the most, only 10% said Facebook. In 2017, Facebook lost around 2.8 million users under 25, and 2018 wasn't much better, say the analysts from *eMarketer*. The only good news is that, worldwide, user stats are still up, and Facebook is expected to continue to grow overall for the next few years. But the loss of popularity among youngsters must be surely causing sleepless nights in Menlo Park.

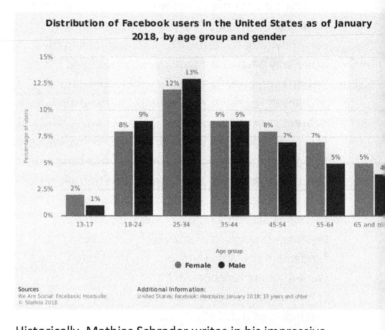

Distribution of Facebook users in the United States as of January 2018, by age group and gender

Historically, Mathias Schrader writes in his impressive book *Transformational Products*, the newsfeed is "the glue between Facebook and its users. That used to be a stream of personal postings from real or Facebook friends – a kind of party line like back in the early days of the telephone, where others could listen in on what you were revealing of yourself. But over time, that too has changed dramatically. Today, newsfeeds are culled from a personalized mix of messages and ads chosen by all-powerful algorithms. According to Pew Research, a full two-thirds (67%) of all adults in the U.S. satisfy their daily news requirements via Facebook exclusively. Only Twitter, which Donald Trump, America's Tweeter in Chief, has chosen as his preferred channel of communication, can make a similar claim: in 2017, the share of users who said that Twitter ws their most important source of news reached 74%! The Reuters Institute of Journalism

found even earlier that the two big Social Web
platforms were eating into cable TV's previous
dominance of the news cycle.

Entertainment channel or media company?

The truth is that it's relatively easy to launch fake
news on the Social Web. Since Facebook continues to
maintain it is not a media company in the traditional
sense, it has been able to avoid being required to
follow the kind quality standards newspapers and
broadcasters are supposed to follow. The Germany,
for instance, the Press Council is tasked with
supervising the media and making sure they stick to a
set of guidelines known as the *Press Codex*. Any news
outlet that oversteps the bounds is required to
publish a retraction or counterstatement or face
humiliating public censure. Were Facebook be held to
the same yardstick it would have to employ slews of
editors and fact checkers. Known in the modern
parlance as "content moderators", these people are
forced to work for little pay doing the dirty work of
spending hours looking at smut and digging into the
roots, factual or not, of fake news. We will discuss
these poop creatures again in a later chapter under
the heading "digital sin eaters".

Up to now, regulators have shied away from imposing
similar constraints on Facebook that they do with
other media companies. To ward off such attempts,
Facebook itself has implemented a slew of measure
to guard against the worse excesses. For instance,
they have published a set of rules their content
moderators are called upon to follow in blocking
content, for instance if "graphic physical abuse",
"hate speech" or "child exploitation". They have also
announced the creation of a kind of appeals court for

users who feel their posts have been blocked unduly. Today, such decisions by Facebook are final. Facebook watchers have long urged greater transparency and giving users a greater say in what is and what isn't deemed appropriate.

Unfortunately, that isn't as easy at is sounds. Different cultural attitudes play a significant role. European, for instance, tend to be more disturbed about depictions of violence that about sexually explicit content. American mores are quite opposite. A good example of this was Facebook's decision to delete the famous photograph taken by star photo journalist Nick Ut of a naked young Vietnamese girl running in tears away from her burning village that had just been set alight by napalm bombs dropped by American forces. The snapshot was voted Press Photo of the Year in 1972, but Facebook banned it. Another famous photo, in which the police chief of Saigon is shown shooting a protester in the head, remained online for months despite vocal protests by Facebook users.

Facebook recently – and more or less reluctantly – agreed to update its community standards and expand its appeals process to allow posters of removed photos, videos or posts to contest determinations they feel were wrongly made. A week after Mark Zuckerberg was grilled on Capitol Hill about Facebook's alleged censorship of conservative viewpoint, the company announced that it was updating its guidelines as part of its CEO's promise to "do better" and be more transparent about how what stays up and what gets taken down.

The question of whether to treat Facebook as a media company or an entertainment channel is especially important in the U.S., where the First

Amendment covers the right to free speech more stringently than in many other democracies, for instance in Europe. The answer will play a big role in determining the course of Facebook's future as a social platform.

One possible solution would be for Facebook to install an *ombud*, or public advocate; an official charged with representing the interests of users by investigating and addressing complaints against the company – an institution that would probably benefit the other members of the GAFA clique, as well. The *Economist* recently weighed in with the idea of creating an international *Data Rights Board* with the power to set guidelines and make sure they are followed. Members of such an institution would probably need to be respected members of the online community who would be given the right to inspect the platforms and their behavior while maintaining strict respect for the privacy of their users.

Of course, human beings would be overtasked with such a job; they will need the assistance of artificial intelligence; system designed to monitor the integrity of their decisions. Scientists at Northeastern University recently proved that Facebook's algorithms routinely pass on personal information such as phone numbers and birthdates to advertisers. A team of researchers at M.I.T. are currently trying to develop a kind of "counter-algorithm" that will sniff out such practices in AI systems. Their solution is something called a "Turning Box"; named after the famous British computer pioneer Alan Turing, this kind of digital portmanteau would be able to test algorithms for hanky-panky and issue a digital seal of quality. Face recognition systems, for instance, could be checked for built-in racial biases that could lead to assigning people to different categories depending on skin color are eye shape. Harvard professor Alan Mislove, who is leading the team of developers, believes his results should be given over to a multinational non-profit organization created as a watchdog to keep an eye on Facebook and others in order to ultimately restore public trust.

Such a system would kill a whole flock of birds with one stone. Facebook is no longer a single corporate enterprise, but a haphazard collection of digital players in a variety of markets. *Facebook Messenger* has more than 1.4 bn users worldwide; just as many use *WhatsApp*, a sister messaging service. The popular photo app *Instagram* is also part of the Facebook empire, as is *Atlas Solutions*, which handles the lion's share of Facebooks advertising revenue. *Oculus VR*, another recent acquisition, builds and markets virtual reality goggles. Masquerade has developed a filter algorithm for selfie pictures and videos which forms an important bridge between Messenger and Instagram. All of these companies form a tight-knit network that is busy exchanging customer data with each other; a fact that Facebook would rather have us forget.

In fact, this data trading is rapidly becoming a major embarrassment for Facebook. In May 2018, the EU Commission forced Facebook to a pay a record fine of €110 m (about $130 m), arguing that Facebook gave misleading information about its habit of sharing user data when it purchased WhatsApp in 2014. At the time, Facebook maintain that this would be technically impossible, but European investigators were able to prove that from the summer of 2016 on, WhatsApp has regularly forwarded details such as phone numbers to its parent company where they form the baisis for targeted ad campaigns. Facebook later admitted the transgressions rather shamefacedly but insisted that it didn't happen "on purpose".

Facebook is a product of the mobile era, even though it looked for a long time as if they were missing the boat on smartphones and other mobile devices. At some point, people in Melo Park woke up, and today Facebook's newsfeed and messenger are two of the most popular mobile apps in the world. Mark Zuckerberg went a step further by acquiring Instagram and WhatsApp, both of which are mobile-only. Through mobile advertising, Facebook is adding billions to its already ample revenue stream.

Facebook is experienced in brazening its way out of tough spots, but one nut still remains to be cracked: China!

After the so-called Ürümqi riots in 2009, which stretched over several days and in which members of the local Uyghur minority in northwestern China clashed with police and regular troops, authorities kicked Facebook and its subsidiaries out of the People's Republic. Chinese users versed in VPN tunneling can still connect to Facebook's servers, but face arrest and jail if found out.

Facebook took eight years to reach its first billion users; the second only took five more years. This means that continuing to grow will be tricky for Facebook without the approximately one billion Internet users in China. At some point, observers believe, Zuckerberg will have to reach some kind of accommodation with the regime in Beijing – and damn the cost! In fact, Facebook's China strategy is becoming increasingly apparent, but it will involve some wrenching changes to its modus operandi. For one, Facebook will have to revert to its original function as a friends' network. It's the newsfeed that the Chinese authorities worry about, so eliminate the new and the problem is solved! This goes a long way to explain the sudden announcement by Facebook in the spring of 2018, which stated that, in order to *"show the right content to the right people at the right time so they don't miss the stories that are important to them", Facebook would concentrate on "organic content", which* refers to the pages of a website that are written and subsequently found primarily by users typing keywords into search engines like Google, Yahoo and Bing. Another word for organic content is personal postings, so increasingly, users get to see content generated by their friends instead of newspapers or magazines. "Personal interaction" is the latest buzzword, and one that will sound reassuring in the ears of Chinese functionaries.

All this came as a shock to advertisers and news media who had grown accustomed to fine-tuning their content to fit the tastes of Facebook users as distilled from their behavior and preferences. This habit, incidentally, led to the rise of "fake news" which became a major factor in the 2016 presidential elections and gave Facebook lots of bad press.

So is the switch to more personal interaction simply Zuckerberg's latest PR strategy aimed at showing Facebook in a better light, or is it part of his long-term plan to pretty his company up in anticipation of reentering the Chinese market? After all, there are plenty of native social media platforms in China like TenCent which boasts about 900 million monthly active users (MAUs) each.

Facebook could learn a lot from TenCent especially, which has pioneered social shopping as well as selling games and music over its platform. Like its competitor WeChat, online payment has become an important business model for TenCent, which operates WeChat Pay. Together with Alibabas Alipay, the two companies handled a staggering $15.4 *trillion* in mobile payments in 2017 – more than 40 times the transactions conducted by smartphone in the U.S.!

The billion-dollar question here is: Will Mark Zuckerberg castrate himself and cave in to the powers that be in Beijing? By cutting himself loose from the newsfeed, he would be going back to his roots, providing nice little notes exchanged between friends with no disturbing content to upset those listening in like people back in the days of the party line. In fact, "party line" would take on a whole new meaning...

When Western Union sent its last telegram over the wires in 2006, there was no big announcement or public commemoration. They simply turned the switch. Presumably, the next major technology facing the same fate is the fixed-line phone.

And what about Facebook? Only time will tell.

Apple, the greedy giant

The historical link between Apple and Standard Oil is so obvious that it scarcely needs pointing out. Both were or are the most valuable companies of their day and age. Both shamelessly exploited or continue to exploit their market dominance to rake in record profits. Both were and and still are in the habit of raising their prices anytime they like - because no one can stop them.

Standard oil paid the price for its rapacity by being broken up by the trust busters. For Apple, that fate may still await.

Apple is the senior member of the GAFA cabal and the only one that is not a purely digital company. However, Apple is the past master in the art of binding people to its platforms, and they will stop at nothing the get there. Like Standard Oil, that gave away lamps in China in order to hook the population on the main product, lamp oil, Apple sells us iPhones and iPads, not because they make that much from the hardware, but because they are a way of hooking us on their many digital services and apps until we are helpless to escape.

Everyone knows that Steve Jobs, who founded the company in 1990 together with his pal Steve Wozniak, was a genius. But nobody who knew him would have ever thought of calling him a nice guy. He was chronically ambitious, lusted for power, drove his people like chattel and tyrannized his customers like no other Silicon Valley boss. The business magazine Fortune ran an article describing his many character faults, upon which Steve rang up the editor and snapped: "Okay, so you found out I'm an asshole. So what else is new?"

And oh, how they loved him for it! When Steve bestrode the stage, the audience erupted like at a Baptist revival meeting. People camped out a day early in order to be first in line for tickets to the Moscone Center in San Francisco, where most of Apple's product launches were held. Once inside, they screamed and shouted, danced around clapping their hands, let out wolf whistles and hugged each other as if it was the Second Coming. In 2001, it was the cool music player iPod that set them off; in 2007

came the iPhone, in 2013 the iPad. And every time it
was a perfectly choreographed spectacle featuring a
slender guy with a three-day beard and a black
turtleneck sweater standing center stage and holding
up for the world to see the Next Big Thing in
techdom.

Jobs, his biographer Walter Isaacsen wrote in 2011,
was a moderately talented engineer, but he was a
ruthless businessman. His biggest coup came when
he founded *iTunes* in 2001 (for once without Apple'
usual ballyhoo) and went on to transform the music
industry in a way that only the invention of the
phonograph had done before. That's because iTunes
isn't a product, but a business model that happens to
combine both hardware and software which not only
plays music, but also organizes your collection and
functions as a music store complete with its very own
payment system.

This wasn't the first time somebody had tried to
distribute music online. The *MP3* format which
shrunk music files down to a size capable of being
transferred over the agonizingly slow Internet of its
day, was developed in 1982 by German scientists at
the Fraunhofer Institute for Integrated Circuits (IIS) in
Erlangen, but became famous through *Napster*, a file
swapping service that soon succumbed to a barrage
of lawsuits fired off by the big music multis. Individual
lables later tried to set up their own download
services, but with small success.

Enter Steve Jobs, who knew most of the music
tycoons personally and persuaded them to allow him
to sell their songs to Apple customers through his
brand-new iTunes online store. At the time, Apple
was a bit player in the PC market (Macs has a market
share in 2001 of about 5%!), so the entertainment

types didn't take him all too seriously. Within a few weeks, Steve managed to sign up every single big label, allowing him to offer their full catalogs on iTunes.

But hardly were the signatures on the contracts dry when sly Steve launched a version of iTunes for Windows – and that for free! Almost overnight, he had created a global market for online music which in turn made his sexy little iPod the hottest thing since sliced bread. The iPod became the most profitable product in Apple's history, far surpassing its computers and laptops. "The iPof was Steve Jobs Trojan Horse", writes Mathias Schrader, "and the hybrid business model became the blueprint for the future."

The iPhone introduced five years later, made Apple the most successful company in the world. In 2015, Apple announced Q1 earnings of $18 bn – the biggest quarterly profit ever made by a public company. In August 2018, Apple hit the $1 trillion market cap, the first company in history to reach that mark. Not even Rockefeller's Standard Oil had ever risen that high!

The parallels between Jobs and Rockefeller go even further, though. The oil magnate was also considered by those who knew him to be ruthless, unscrupulous and greedy. The economic historian Robert Whaples once described his business methods like this: "somehow he managed to bully and connive his way to a position of dominance", while admitting that he achieved this through "relentless cost cutting and efficiency improvements, boldness in betting on the long-term prospects of the industry while others were willing to take quick profits, and impressive abilities to spot and reward talent, delegate tasks, and manage a growing empire."

Sounds just like Steve Jobs, doesn't it?

At its height, Rockefeller's Standard Oil controlled 90% of crude oil production in the United States. He also bought up railways to transport his oil around the country, and in 1902 he branched out into coal mining. For this, his name will ever be associated with what became known as the "Ludlow Massacre" which occurred when scabs burned down a tent village where striking coal workers and their families had taken refuge, resulting in the burning deaths of 13 women and children.

Nevertheless, Rockefeller continues to enjoy a shining reputation as one of America's leading philanthropists. The son of a deeply pious Baptist family, Rockefeller grew up in a culture of charitable giving, and over the course of his lifetime he is estimated to have given away more than $500 m. Most observers believe, however, that his generosity was triggered for the most part by the mounting pressure brought against him and his company by the ant-trust authorities and President Teddy Roosevelt which led in 1911 to the Supreme Court's decision to break up his monopoly into 34 independent oil companies.

For Rockefeller, this proved to be a benefit in disguise. Many of the new corporations with names such as *ConocoPhillips*, *Amoco* (which today belongs to *BP*), *Chevron* and *ExxonMobile* remain among the leading petrochemical giants of the world, and their value soon rose fivefold. Rockefeller, who had kept a stake in each of them, was soon worth more than $900 m which, converted to today's dollars – would put him on par with the richest men in the world like Bill Gates, Warren Buffet or Jeff Bezos.

His biographer Ron Chernow, who called Rockefeller the "Jekyll-and-Hyde of American capitalism", wrote: "his good side was every bit as good as his bad side was bad... He was arrogant. He saw his every action as a gift to the world. Sometimes he was right, and sometimes he was dreadfully wrong." Seldom has history brought forth such a contradictory figure – at least until Steven Jobs came along.

Steve was hardly under the ground before the first so-called *iShrines* began popping up all over the Web; the digital equivalents of wayside crosses where his fans could glorify his vision and management style in ways reminiscent of the veneration of medieval saints. Apple aficionados held midnight vigils in front of Apple Stores in New York, San Francisco and London. In an attempt to tamp down the burgeoning Jobs Mania, techno-blogger Liam Alexander wrote: "Jobs the man was arrogant, selfish and ruthless. These traits may have helped him on his way to the top, but they didn't make him especially loveable for those around him. He was constantly demanding more and more of his people, and those who fell short were often driven to tears."

Okay, he suffered his share of setbacks which may explain his toughness with himself and others. In 2004, he was forced by pressure from investors to reveal that he was suffering from liver cancer, but instead of seeking qualified medical help he insisted on putting himself in the hands of quacks and alternative therapists before finally admitting shortly before he died that it had probably been his greatest mistake.

For Jobs as for Rockefeller it can be said that, if they had stuck to the rules probably nobody would have cared how big a jerk they were. In the case of

Standard Oil, this was evidently not the case, which led to one of the most spectacular anti-trust proceedings in economic history. What the consequences for Apple will be remains to be seen.

An antifragile monopoly

Despite its reputation as the inventor of the modern smartphone, Apple's market share is only 15%, and the company had to watch helplessly as Samsung breezed by them in 2018. But this hasn't stopped USB analyst Steven Milunovich describing Apple as an "antifragile monopoly".

The term "antifragile" was coined by the Lebanese–American essayist, economist and statistician Nassim Nicholas Taleb, who divides the world and everything in it into three categories: the fragile, the robust and the antifragile. Being fragile means you try to avoid disorder and disruption because of the mess they might make of your life; in fact, though you are making yourself vulnerable to the shock that will tear everything apart. Being robust means you can stand up to shocks without changing who you are. Being antifragile means that disruption makes you stronger and more creative, better able to adapt to new challenges. Taleb thinks we should all try to be antifragile.

Milunovich accuses Apple of setting price levels for smartphones through its public perception as the dominant player in the makret, even though that isn't strictly true. "Monopolies typically control pricing for the entire product category. An iPhone today costs $700 on average, and Apple manages to maintain or even raise this level despite currency fluctuations and pressure from its competitors. Others are forced to sell by reducing their prices; Apple doesn't need to. As a result, Apple's share of smartphone profits globally is disproportionately high, namely about 80%."

In the days of Standard Oil and the Railroad Barons, anti-trust law was unequivocal: Monopoly protection meant preventing individual companies or groups of companies from exploiting the position to push competitors out, enabling them to raise prices unfairly, which damaged both individual consumers and the market as a whole. In Apple's case, it's the other way around: Having created a "platform", Apple can actively invite third parties to develop Apps and applications, but only under strict supervision by Apple which argues that it is only maintaining its high quality standards. In reality, it reserves its ability to refuse access to the platform to competitors for whatever reason. And as for prices: the cost of distributing copies of digital originals tends towards zero.

If you read the fine print in existing anti-trust legislation, however, you discover that one of the lawmakers' declared aims was to prohibit companies from abusing a monopoly position. It seems abundantly clear that the strategy Apple is following is intended to stop competitors getting too close and skimming off too much cream – a classic case of monopoly abuse. At least that's what Glenn Manishin believes. An attorney working for the law firm Duane Morris in Philadelphia, Manishin was involved in the breakup of AT&T in 1985 and went on to advise various industrial associations in their anti-trust campaigns against Microsoft in 1998. He freely admits that Apple has earned its monopoly position for its operating system iOS fairly and squarely by building "insanely good products". He worries, however, that

Apple is regularly using its dominance to cut competitors off. "These are methods that go far beyond anything Microsoft used to do in the old days of Netscape and others in the pre-digital era of the 1990ies", we wrote.

He lists a litany of unfair practices by Apple, including secret price fixing agreements with the five biggest U.S. publishers intended to inflate the price of eBooks. Amazon used to charge $9.99 per electronic copy, but Apple and its willing coterie of booksellers managed to drive that up to $14.99. In March 2016, a U.S. court sentenced Apple and its gang to a fine of $450 m. In another case, it turned out that Apple was putting the thumbscrews on competitors like *Spotify*, *Pandora*, and *Rhapsody* by demanding a 30% commission every time a user signed up for their services through the Apple store, forcing them to raise their own prices. And to this day, Apple refuses to allow app developers to redirect buyers to their own websites, where the same product is usually available at a much lower price. These companies are actually prohibited to mention the fact on their homepages!

Experts have long believed that Apple is using secret, undocumented interfaces to ensure its proprietary music service, *Apple Music*, is given exclusive access to additional functions provided by its popular chatbot, *Siri*. And Apple has been shown to install links in song files that automatically redirect users to its own streaming service. Manishin draws a direct parallel to *American Express'* habit of forbidding dealers to inform customers about more attractive conditions offered by competitors like *Visa* or *MasterCard* – a practice that led in 2013 to a court verdict in the U.S. declaring Amexco to be in defiance of the Sherman Act and other anti-trust regulations.

Since 2016, the Federal Trade Commission FTC has been investigating Apple because of its suspicious business behavior in dealing with competing streaming operators, hitherto without tangible results. Given the unwillingness of the current administration to take its oversight obligations against banks and other corporations seriously, it is likely that Apple will go off scott free. In a statement Spotify's CEO Daniel Ek complained that ""Apple has long used its control of iOS to squash competition in music. You know something's wrong when Apple makes more from selling Spotify accounts than through their own contracts with the music industry", he complained. "Apple doesn't want to share with the music industry – it wants to have its cake and eat it, too!"

In 2016, Liberal senator Elizabeth Warren hit out at the tech industry in a new speech railing against consolidation and concentration in the American economy. "Google, Apple, and Amazon provide platforms that lots of other companies depend on for survival", she said. "But Google, Apple, and Amazon also, in many cases, compete with those same small companies, so that the platform can become a tool to snuff out competition."

In the summer of 2018, there was no end in sight to the FTC investigation against Apple, but the storm clouds were definitely gathering over the company's headquarters in Cupertino. When and how the storm will break appears to be only a matter of time. But one thing is certain: Apple and the other tech giants are heading for trouble.

Of FAANGs and ANTs

Until now, this chapter has been all about the "Big Four", or GAFA as they are known collectively. This is because Google, Amazon, Facebook and Apple have been playing in a league of their own until recently, dominating their respective core markets in ways that make it seem impossible for any serious competitor to arise anytime soon. Besides, all four share a certain nefariousness as well as the ability to focus tightly on the one thing that counts for them, namely raking in obscene profits regardless of the cost to society. The term "greed capitalism" could have been coined specially for them, and unless forced to, they disregard all norms of civilized commerce, fair business practices and even basic human decency.

Of course there are loads of companies that play in the second division, so to speak: *Uber* (ride sharing), *AirBnB* (hospitality, *Plantir* (Big Data) or *WeWork* (co-working) spring to mind; all of them belong to the rare species of *Decacorns* – companies that have managed to achive a market capitalization of ten billion dollars or more. It seems doubtful, however, that any of them will one day manage to rise to play with the really big boys. At the end of the day, they are niche players (big niche players, admittedly) in their separate fields, but they hardly effect the everyday lives of billions of people in the way the GAFAs do. Hard to imagine life in the digital age without Google; without Uber, life would go on.

So if we want to look for possible successors to GAFA we need to turn to the East. Chris Skinner, a journalist and financial consultant, wrote in *thefinancier.com*: "Forget GAFA, the real threat is FATBAG!"

The abbreviation stands for *Facebook, Amazon, TenCent, Baidu, Ant* and *Google* and thus for a kind of Gang of Six that include the three most powerful Internet companies in China.

Baidu is China's Google and has recently made the list of the five most heavily trafficked websites in the world. Like its U.S. counterpart, Baidu is at home in many different markets, from music downloads and AI to self-driving cars and busses. Criticism of Baidu centers around its willingness to blindly obey the powers that be in the Middle Kingdom. *Reporters Without Borders*, a human rights organization, accuses Baidu of systematically purging its search engine of "subversive" content.

Baidu has developed an operating system of its own called *Apollo*, that uses voice control and artificial intelligence. Baidu seems intent on establishing Apollo as the "Android of the automobile industry", and it has signed an agreement with BMW as a major step towards this end, so watch what you say when at the wheel; Beijing is probably listening!

Ma Huateng, also known as Pony Ma, the richest man in China according to Forbe's World Billionaires list, founded TenCent, Chinas equivalent to Facebook – except that TenCent can do a lot more than Facebook! Ma's company operates one of the world's leading game platforms; its smash hit, *Honor of Kings*, draws more than 80 million gamers a day. TenCent Music, which runs the music portals *QQ Music*, *KuGou*, and *Kuwo*, dominates the Chinese market. Reportedly, Ma is currently investing heavily in artificial intelligence technology with the aim of further improving his existing services as well as enabling new ones. TenCent's messenger app, *WeChat*, and its online payment app far surpass Facebook in their ability to handle online payments, which in China is on the verge of replacing cash as the accepted way of paying for everything from restaurant tabs to groceries or newspapers, not to mention billions of online transactions.

Ant Financial is a subsidiary of Alibaba, a huge conglomerate founded in 1999 by Jack Ma, a former English instructor, who recently stepped down as chairman and CEO to enjoy his fabulous wealth. With turnover exceeding 40 billion dollars a year, Alibaba is considered the "Amazon of China". Ant, on the other hand, is the parent company of *Alipay*, which last year was responsible for online payments totaling more than eight trillion (!) dollars; half of all online transactions in China. This compares with the measly 155 billion handled by its nearest U.S. competitor, *PayPal*.

Another abbreviation making the rounds among stock broker since late 2017 is *FAANG*, which was coined by Jim Cramer, the host of CNBC's program *Mad Money*. *He* adds a fifth tech giant to the four usual suspects, namely *Netflix* – an interesting choice!

To use an analogy every fan of *Star Wars* will understand immediately, Facebook, Amazon, Apple and Google represent the dark side of the force, while Netflix is like *Chewbacca*, the big, clumsy, lovable bear who flies spaceships and is fondly known as "Chewie". While the other online mammoths are constantly being accused in the headlines of exploiting their users' data, dodging taxes, abusing their monopoly powers and being the digital equivalent of drug dealers, everyone loves Netflix – although in fact Netflix dominates its market just as effectively as Amazon does online commerce or Facebook dos the Social Web. Since its founding in 1997, Netflix has fundamentally transformed television. The company began life in DVD rental but sooner than others recognized the huge potential of streaming video, which it pioneered, creating a whole new market. Writing in June 2018, the *Economist* described Netflix as "the world's first global TV powerhouse". But unlike GAFA, Netflix made it to the top without incurring public protests, much less threats of increased government supervision.

One reason is that no one in the past seems to have taken Netflix seriously. The big media companies slept through the streaming video revolution just like newspaper publishers remained largely ignorant of the opportunities the World Wide Web was offering. As a result, the majors were willing to hand over their digital video content to Netflix for peanuts in the beginning. Now, they need to scramble to catch up with Netflix or at least stay in the race. The recent megadeals such as the takeover of *Time Warner* by *AT&T* or the vicious bidding war between *Comcast* and *Walt Disney* over the pay TV channel *Sky* are best seen against this background.

The other tech giants are busy studying the rise of Netflix to understand how they managed to keep out of the limelight. One reason is that Netflix itself has stayed away from the news-gathering business, choosing to remain a harmless peddler of entertainment for the masses. At no time has Netflix's name been associated with things like Fake News or election tampering. And unlike Google or Facebook, who rely on advertising for the lion's share of their revenues, Netflix has remained true to its old-fashioned subscription model. That means they don't have to persuade users to hand over their personal data or sell their attention to the highest bidder.

GAFA are unmistakably American companies, but Netflix has managed to transform itself into a truly international entity with TV shows airing in 21 countries and in dozens of languages around the globe. They now have more subscribers outside America than inside it. "Other tech firms can learn from Netflix to use data with greater care, to be clearer about the terms of trade with their customers and to be more respectful of local markets", the *Economist* counseled. Whether the present crop of GAFAs will take that lesson to heart remains to be seen

Chapter 3: How to fix the Internet

"Those who cannot learn from history are doomed to repeat it."

George Santayana

The Web needs fixing, that is clear. We can't afford to sit around watching as huge internet companies seize more power than ever before in corporate history, amass riches beyond measure and shape the fate of society and of humankind to fit their own agendas. Like the Robber Barons in the final days of the Wild West, they need to be reined in and taken to task, one laborious step at a time. We – consumers, citizens, voters – will have to force them to play by the rules, and where there are no rules we need to write new ones. But what will the new playbook contain and how can GAFA & Co. be compelled to follow it?

In my humble opinion, there are basically four means at our disposal to fix the Web and make sure the Digital Society is one we all are willing to be part of:

1. **Regulation**: "Law & order" in the parlance of the Wild West. We need to examine our existing laws and make sure they are suited to the new reality; if not, we need to make ones that are. It would be best if these new rules were applicable all over the world, but if authoritarian states like China and Russia refuse to cooperate, the democratic societies need to close ranks and resist. Europe will play an important role here, but even getting the 28 EU member states to sing from the same song sheet has proven in the past to be about as tough as herding cats. Yet, we have no other choice! Thankfully, society has been there before, and we can learn from history. The big shifts at the end of the 19th century, when the first anti-trust laws were passed, health and safety regulations were established, and civil rights defined and enforced, were equally transformational. Remember: It took until 1911 before the first successful anti-trust lawsuit was won and Standard Oil broken up under the terms of the Sherman Act, which Congress had agreed on 16 years previously in 1890.

2. **Technology**: "Technologies are morally neutral until we apply them", writes Gerd Leonhard in his book *Technology vs. Humanity*. It all depends on how we use them. If it is true that Silicon Valley has brought us things like data theft, digital

heteronomy, fake news, trolls, hate postings, information overload and total transparency, then the same technology ought to be able to help us overcome its own worst excesses. If, as Sebastian Halm writes in *iBusiness*, a newsletter, that sexist bots and racist artificial intelligence exist, then it is because of biased algorithms that reflect the prejudices of their programmers; that means it should be possible to create antisexist and antiracist algorithms, too. All it takes is the willingness to do so. We need to remind the tech giants of their social responsibility and demand that they follow principles we can all agree on. And they will need to cough up the necessary funds for the development of technologies whose aim is to abolish the aberrations the Wild Wild Web has wrought.

3. **Market power**: Never in history have consumers been so empowered. The internet has brought about an unparalleled freedom and breadth of choice as well as a world-wide communications system that enables us to share our experiences with vendors and products in a manner never seen before. This includes the ability to complain to others about unfair or antisocial company behavior and to muster support against the perpetrators. The Web has taught us a new word – shitstorm – to describe this collective outburst of rage and vituperation. "In the Age of the Internet, the customer is truly king", I wrote as far back as 2002 in my book *The Customer Cartel*. And we aren't talking a hapless and harmless constitutional monarch here by any means; instead, his Majesty can at times be a true tyrant. If the digital giants

persist in putting profit and market share before their civic and social responsibilities, it will be up to us to unleash our newfound collective prepotency against them until they mend their ways. "We are the people", crowds chanted on the streets of East Germany in the autumn of 1989, causing the party bigwigs to tremble and the Wall to fall. "We are the online market" would be a good idea for a new slogan in the Age of the Internet.

4. **Self-help**: When the internet was young, conversations among users mostly happened in forums or in the Usenet. The tone there was rough: So-called "flame wars" were frequent; acrimonious "rage postings" were the norm. Users are prone to besiege each other with taunts and personal abuses. It was then that the idea of a "netiquette" became popular; a set of rules governing accepted online behavior. None of them had any legal validity, but they were popular and widespread, and they at least helped to tone down some of the most vehement online clashes. In 2010, the German Knigge Council, named after the famous German Count Adolph von Knigge, whose rules of etiquette, published in in 1788, was one of the best-known works of the Enlightenment, a treatise on social skills called "Über den Umgang mit Menschen " (translated as "Practical Philosophy of Social Life"), published a set of "politeness rules" covering most aspects of coexistence in the Age of the Internet. And why not? If most of us agree what represents obnoxious online behavior, we might also be able to adopt countermeasures that are

binding for all. Lock out the thugs! In a world of total communication, being ignored is quite possible the worst punishment imaginable. We just have to agree on what constitutes bad manners. All it takes is a little digital common sense!

The object of this chapter is to examine how existing rules and regulations effect the World Wide Web and ask ourselves whether we need new laws in order to fix the internet or if the old ones are sufficient. Do we need more or fewer regulations? Can creativity and spontaneity survive the heavy hand of the regulators or will they be stifled by regimentation? And anyway, what does "rule of law" mean in a virtual world where life goes on behind the computer screen? But above all, how can we force GAFA and their henchmen to clean up their acts and abide by rules that are made for all?

Of right and might

The Wild Wild Web ended officially on May 18, 2018. On this day, the British Secretary of State for Digital, Culture, Media and Sport, Matt Hancock, declared in an interview with the *Daily Telegraph* of London that the "'Wild West era for technology firms like Facebook and Google is over." Silicon Valley giants, he warned, must face much greater regulation to control their use of people's data and ensure they cannot avoid being properly taxed.

By drawing the historic parallel between the Wild West and the modern digital reality, Hancock was echoing a widespread misbelief, namely that the World Wide Web represents a legal vacuum and that it is therefore the job of politicians to curb the greatest excrescences and establish the rule of cyberlaw.

What do they mean by "legal vacuum"? Do they really believe that there is such a place and that the long arm of the law can't touch them when they're online? What balderdash! Of course, every single statute on the books is as valid in cyberspace as it is in our homes and on our streets. Of course, there is always the problem of making the law work, but that applies everywhere. The real problem is geography: The World Wide Web is impossible to locate; it knows no boundaries and national borders, which makes it especially difficult to win one's case.

In the Wild West, that job usually fell to the sheriff or marshal if he happened to be in town. Wanted posters issued in one part of the country had to be distributed and displayed over a wide area, but the bad guys were usually brought to justice eventually. Most ruffians ended like Butch Cassidy and Billy the Kid.

Over the short history of the internet politicians have made many attempts at bending the World Wide Web to their wills. From data retention to intellectual property or kiddie porn, lobbyists and populists are fond of bemoaning the lack of norms and means to crackdown on what they feel are digital loopholes in the legal system. Untrue, rights activists retort; the other side is stifling the Web through excessive regulation and creating an Orwellian surveillance state by keeping constant watch on its citizens when they're online.

"The babble about legal vacuums distracts from the real problems", Konrad Lischka wrote as early as 2009 in *Spiegel Online*. In fact, there are more than enough regulations that cover the internet that were created solely for that purpose. The result, he believes, has been a hodgepodge of laws and statutes of varying quality that courts have interpreted in very different ways. As a result, the authorities are often reluctant to apply them at all.

Both sides are on to something: The legal framework within which the Web operates is in fact flimsy and badly in need of bolstering. One reason is the borderless nature of the Web which makes a demarcation line seem superannuated, leading to endless arguments about jurisdiction. Does the law of the country in which a transaction is initiated apply, or should the laws of the State of California apply all over the world just because three out of four GAFA companies happen to be headquartered there? Or how about Washington State, where both Amazon and Microsoft reside? The GAFA lawyers like to point out that anybody who uses one of their online services has by necessity agreed to their terms and conditions, which contain a reference to the legal venue users must submit to. The EU adopted the "land of origin principle" for electronic commerce back in 2000 to ensure that a company setting up, for instance, in Italy will be judged according to Italian law, even if it sells to a customer in, say, France or Germany. At the same time, the European Union embraces the so-called "consuming country principle", which means that local consumer protection laws apply every time someone purchases something online.

The online taxman cometh

In the US, the Supreme Court decided in June 2018 to end the decades-old custom of freeing online vendors from paying local sales taxes. The exception dates back to the very early days of e-commerce, when lawmakers were worried about stalling online sales, which anyway made up only a tiny fraction of the gross domestic product. Ignoring online may have made sense at the time, but with Amazon alone accounting for 15% of trade volume in the US and Germany and 17% in the UK, the situation has changed dramatically. According to the World Trade Organization (WTO), more than two billion consumers will be buying goods and services online by 2021, generating a turnover of more than $4 billion. Since Amazon handles at least half of this huge sum either directly or through its third-party partners on the Amazon Marketplace, it is obvious that governments all over the world want to get their hands in the till.

In Europe, the EU has announced changes to its existing VAT regulations starting in 2020 leading to uniform rates for sales taxes throughout the EU. Austria wants to introduce its own version of a "digital tax" which will ignore the country of origin principle by taxing transactions at the local level. This will mean that Facebook, for example, will be required to pay taxes on income paid by Austrian advertisers.

Copyright is for publishers, not authors

Politicians aren't internet experts, as a rule – and that makes them so dangerous. Nowhere is this more apparent than in the endless squabbling over copyright protection. Historically, the idea of protecting someone's intellectual property is quite a recent invention. While contract and ownership laws in most Western countries date back to Roman times or to even more ancient tribal laws, the need to regulate the right to reproduce content only arose with Johannes Guttenberg's invention of the printing press in 1453. In those days, authors were only paid for delivering their work to the printer, who could do whatever he wanted with it.

Authors' privileges are an invention of the European Renaissance in 16the century. In 1511, Albrecht Dürer was granted the right to be recognized as the creator of his famous etchings by Emperor Maximilian I. In England, printers organized in the "Stationers' Company" were granted the exclusive right to reproduce books in the *Statute of Anne* which was passed by parliament in 1710. Only guild members were recognized as "copy owners", and their "copy right" ensured that only they were allowed to produce copies of books and pamphlets. Copyright, from the very beginning, was for publishers, not authors – and that hasn't changed one little bit.

If you thought pirate copies were an invention of the Internet Age, think again! William Shakespeare complained bitterly about copyists who would sit in the audience during performances of his plays and write down everything that was said onstage. Scrupulous printers would run off a few hundred copies within days of opening night. Cheap "quarto" editions of famous plays such as *Romeo and Juliette*, *Macbeth* or *Hamlet* sold well, but the Bard of Avon never saw a farthing.

When the Wild West was at its height, the English author Charles Dickens ran into similar trouble with American publishers, who produced rip-off versions of his bestsellers such as *David Copperfield* or *Oliver Twist*, selling millions of copies without paying any royalties. Dickens became so frustrated that he went on tour in 1842, traveling the length of the East Coast with his wife Catherine, where he rented large halls and held readings from his works, for which the public had to purchase tickets. His expedition was a smash success and largely compensated him for the losses from missed royalty payments on the other side of the Atlantic.

Maybe Dickens was ahead of his time. In the digital world, after all, there is no telling original and copy apart; they both consist of the same bits and bytes. Musician nowadays rely increasingly on live concerts for their livings. Recordings, CDs, and media streams are a way to become better known and sell tickets.

Information want to be free of charge

So, it pays to adapt to changing times. Unfortunately, that is something most newspaper publishers failed to grasp. At least that seems to be the only possible explanation for their stringent demands for ancillary copyrights in Europe.

The publisher's business model used to be straightforward: The publisher paid writers and reporters. The results were promulgated in paper form or later online, which most publishers only saw as way to recycle the content they had already run in their newspapers and magazines and which they gave away for free. Finding a way to make online pay for itself baffled most publishers, who never really understood what a powerful competitor it could one day become. Readers, of course, were happy to consume online news without paying, and anyway, the motto in the early days of the internet was "information wants to be free". Most people assumed this to mean "free of charge" and were quite happy with it.

But then search engines like Google, Bing or Yahoo! started mining this motherload of free content for tiny "snippets", which they used to draw online readers and thus become news mongers themselves. Since the snippets were linked to the publishers' websites, this was considered fair practice, and, in fact, most news outlets began to rely on the steady stream of traffic brought their way by the search engines without them having to lift a finger.

This giveaway culture worked well for both sides – as long as publishers could get by selling advertising for their online news sites. But as targeted online marketing through things like Google AdWords took off, the publisher's advertising revenue started drying up while Google and others began to rake in billions. Somebody eventually had the bright idea to ask politicians to force the search companies to share their bonanza by paying for the right to publish snippets linked to their news.

Let's pause for a moment here and consider what this means. Imagine a taxi driver who is in the habit of taking his passengers to the best bars, restaurants and shops in town where they spend lots of money. The taxi driver doesn't do this out of the goodness of his heart, but because it makes his own customers happy and he gets lots of tips. The shop owners, on the other hand, get lots of extra revenue, so they're happy too. Got it so far?

Now imagine the shop owner suddenly realizes that the taxi driver is making money by chauffeuring his passengers to their stores, so they start demanding a cut of his profits. And since the guy's just a dumb slob of a taxi driver anyway, and the shop owners have friends in high places, they persuades his politician buddies to pass a law forcing the taxi driver to fork out every time he brings in a new customer. Still got it?

I didn't either, at first. After all, why should the taxi driver continue to ferry customers to the store owners? And why should Google keep sending readers to the publisher's websites if they have to pay for the privilege? The whole idea is so wildly bizarre that you would imagine no rational person would consider it for a minute.

Unfortunately, the majority of European parliamentarians apparently are irrational. On September 12, 2018, the so-called Ancillary Copyright Bill was passed along with along with a law requiring online companies like Google or YouTube to install so-called "content filters" that automatically stop users from downloading or viewing copyrighted material such as texts, images, and videos. Activists say that this will mean the end of the internet as we know it; a freewheeling marketplace of ideas and memes open to all.

And as for the publishers: They will reap what they have sowed. It doesn't take a great leap of the imagination to predict how Google and the others will react, namely by ceasing to publish snippets linked to newspapers and magazines. Publishers will lose their most important source of new readers, more newspapers will close, diversity of opinion on which democratic societies depend will wither and die. The 12th of September will go down in history as a black day for liberal society and the Web.

The Spanish mystic St. Theresa of Avila (1515-1582) is supposed to have warned: "There are more tears shed over prayers that are answered than over those that go unanswered." Be careful what you pray for: publishers and politicians have yet to learn this simple lesson.

How could they? After all, the current generation of politicians are generally digital neophytes who grew up long before the internet. Asking them to regulate cyberspace is like asking a Catholic priest to give sex education. Unfortunately, politicians in general tend to enjoy interfering with things they know nothing about. In the case of the World Wide Web, this means the less regulation the better!

Why we need a digital Sherman Act

One area where we will need the help of politicians is the necessary reform of our anti-trust laws that are completely inadequate for reigning in GAFA and other internet monopolists. It is past time for an update – a digital edition of the Sherman Act.

In Western society, virtually all anti-trust legislation can be traced back to a bill introduced on July 2, 1890 by John Sherman, a Republican Senator, and backed nearly unanimously by both houses of Congress and aimed at preventing the artificial raising of prices by restriction of trade or supply. So-called "innocent monopolies" achieved solely by merit remained legal but acts by a monopolist to artificially preserve that status, or nefarious dealings to create a monopoly, were not. In other words, the Sherman Act was not intended to impact market gains obtained by honest means, by benefiting the consumers more than the competitors.

Historically, the Sherman Act was aimed at the Robber Barons of the Gilded Age – the capitalist titans who held great industrial monopolies and unprecedented wealth while children worked in factories and whole regions of the country were stuck in poverty after the Civil War. The drafters of the law were especially concerned with the railroad barons and sugar cartels, but in fact the act was first put to the test in 1906 in the case against Standard Oil. The company had been established in 1870 by John D. Rockefeller; it later became an innovator in the development of the business trust through both horizontal and vertical integration: Standard Oil bought up most of its direct competitors, but also branched out into refining and logistics until, by 1904, controlled some 91% of production and 85% of final sales in America. On its way, "Big Oil" become the richest company the world was to ever see until Apple took the crown in 2018. According the government, Standard stood accused of raising prices to its monopolistic customers but lowering them to hurt competitors, often disguising its illegal actions by using bogus supposedly independent companies it controlled. On May 15, 1911, the Supreme Court upheld lower court judgments and declared Standard Oil to be an "unreasonable" monopoly. It ordered the company to be broken up into 34 independent companies with different boards of directors.

In a sense, the Sherman Act was the result of the First Industrial Revolution; it was intended to limit price fixing and abuse of market power. But it has proven astonishingly flexible over the years. Cases have been brought against monopolistic practices in big-league sports, in the film industry, and in telecommunications. In one of the most spectacular anti-trust suits in US history, the government went after AT&T, whom they accused of stifling competition. In 1984, agreement was reached and "Ma Bell", as the company was nicknamed, was forced to spin off its local telephone business into seven so-called Regional Bell Operating Companies, instantly christened "Baby Bells" in everyday parlance. The mother ship retained its monopoly on long distance calls along with the Yellow Pages, Bell Labs and the iconic bell-shaped trademark.

The Bell breakup, by the way, marked the last time the Sherman Act was used to combat so-called vertical mergers – a combination of buyer and supplier. Since then, courts have developed what the *New York Times* recently called a "laissez-faire approach to vertical mergers". In attempting to put the brakes on the merger of Fruehauf, the country's largest manufacturer of truck trailers, and Kelsey-Hayes, a maker of heavy-duty wheels and antiskid systems, the government lost its case.

Legal experts believe that this major mind shift in the '70s and '80s is due to an essay penned in 1978 by Robert H. Bork, a former solicitor general and Supreme Court nominee (never confirmed), who argued in "The Antitrust Paradox" that the purpose of trust busting was to protect customers by encouraging economic efficiencies. Vertical mergers, he said, do exactly that und should therefore be exempt from government interference. For instance, in June 2018, Richard J. Leon, the federal judge in charge of the decision to permit the $85 billion merger between AT&T and Time Warner, embraced the Bork argument that a firm's dominance in one market cannot be leveraged into another, and that success in the market is determined by the good it brings to the customer. Vertical markets, Leon argued, are more efficient, and these efficiencies can be passed onto the customer in the form of lower prices, higher quality or both.

But in recent years, more antitrust experts have questioned the laissez-faire approach to vertical merger enforcement, especially in cases involving media and private data. They believe we need to rethink the way we deal with corporate power. So, do we need a new Sherman Act for the Digital Age, one capable of taming GAFA and making them behave? That conclusion is hard to escape.

In May 2015, Prof. Frank Pasquale of the University of Maryland published an essay in the journal *American Affairs* entitled "Tech Platforms and the Knowledge Problem", which caused a mild sensation in anti-trust circles. In it, he quotes the Austrian economist Friedrich August von Hayek (1899-1992) who maintained that planned socialist economies failed because of the lack of knowledge. In "Taylorized" manufacturing based on the division of labor, individual planners can no longer oversee the entire process in detail, he wrote. No person can know everything about how goods and services interact and move in an economy. Hayek called this "distributed knowledge."

"In an era of artificial intelligence and mass surveillance, however, the possibility of central planning has reemerged—this time in the form of massive firms", Pasquale maintains. Having logged and analyzed billions of transactions, Amazon knows intimate details about all its customers and suppliers, he says. "It can carefully calibrate screen displays to herd buyers toward certain products or shopping practices, or to copy sellers with its own, cheaper, in-house offerings." Also, Amazon has been shown to manipulate law and contracts to accumulate unfair advantages.

Similarly, Google not only knows that customers are searching for, but also what other companies are searching for, buying, emailing, and planning and can match the data it gathers from the raw flow of communication it monitors.

"The rise of powerful intermediaries like search engines and insurers may seem like the next logical step in the development of capitalism. But a growing chorus of critics questions the size and scope of leading firms in these fields", Pasquale states. Consumer advocates, he says, have long accused Google of manipulating advertising on its website, but lacking legal leverage, it will be hard – but maybe not impossible – to force them to change their ways.

"Can these diverse strands of protest and critique coalesce into something more durable and consistent?", Pasquale asks. In his eyes, GAFA are data monopolists whose power far exceeds that of Standard Oil in its heyday. Governments and societies will eventually be forced to take action, he believes. In fact, that is already happening as we speak. In 2017, the anti-trust department of the European Union posed a record fine of $2.4 billion on Google for unfairly ranking its own search results higher than those of its competitors. This is at least a first step, but more will need to follow. We will discuss Europe's possible leadership role in creating a digital New Deal at the end of this chapter.

The biggest problem, according to Pasquale, will be to get two competing schools of thought to agree on a common solution. In his essay, he takes us back to Thomas Jefferson, who concluded the Louisiana Purchase that effectively marked the beginning of the Wild West. Jefferson was a fan of states' rights and "small government". His biggest opponent was Alexander Hamilton, the main author of the Federalist Papers and a proponent of a strong central administration, who somehow morphed into the star of a famous Broadway musical. He has often been described as the father of "big government". The war of ideas between the two continues to this day, with

Democrats mostly following the Hamiltonian tradition and Republicans endorsing Jefferson's positions.

Pasquale describes the "Jefferson/Hamilton divide" in anti-trust policies. This became especially apparent at a conference sponsored in the spring of 2018 by the Booth School of Business at the University of Chicago, a hotbed of Jeffersonian thinking about the role of the state. The meeting dealt with questions of internet regulation, data ownership, informational self-determination, and the addictive effects social web as a health hazard. It was suggested that a supervisory body should be created under the aegis of the World Trade Union, its members to be drawn from all walks of life and many different areas of business and science.

The proposals put forward in Chicago can be categorized along the Jefferson/Hamilton divide:

- For instance, a member of the Hamilton school criticized the administration for waving through the acquisition by Facebook of WhatsApp and Instagram and demanded that the megadeal be rescinded. They called for measures to prohibit Google from manipulating search results to harm its competitors, and Amazon should be forced by the government to compete with their own customers on the Amazon Marketplace. Lina Khan form the Open Markets Institute suggested that anti-trust statues similar to those that regulate the financial sector and the railroads should apply.
- Jeffersonians made a strong case for voluntary self-regulation and restrained use of government authority. Their proposals included "data sharing" and the development

of interfaces designed to guarantee data portability, an idea geeks like to call "regulation by API": open programming interfaces, they maintained, would allow other market players including small startups to access data streams, enabling them to compete with GAFA on equal terms.

At the symposium, Viktor Mayer-Schönberger, an Austrian legal scholar and head of the Oxford Internet Institute, introduced his concept of "mandatory data exchange" that, he felt, should be linked to company size. The mandate should kick in at 10% of market share, he suggested; after that, internet companies should be compelled to share customer feedback, thus creating a level playing field for smaller companies and ensuring that innovation isn't stifled by GAFA's predominance.

Naturally, the Jefferson and Hamilton camps arrived at vastly different conclusions about how to fix the internet. For Jeffersonians, the answer to Google is breakup! Google's parent company Alphabet should be prohibited from acquiring any additional small companies. Similarly, Facebook should be dismantled since nobody believed its claims to have introduced effective solutions since 2014 to guard against reoccurrence of the Cambridge Analytica mess. In fact, conference attendees maintained, Facebook has gone further, if anything, to increase its stranglehold on its users' personal data, thus holding down any possible competitor.

Hamiltonians, on the other hand, argue that strong companies like Facebook with large, centralized data bases actually reduce the risk of data theft, but only if Facebook is placed under strong government supervision. Facebook, they claimed, is no different than any other media company or broadcaster, and they should be held accountable for any fake news distributed over their network. This would include a right of reply like any other press organ. Facebook, of course, is unwilling to shoulder the expected costs, so regulation appears to be the only option. And in fact, Mark Zuckerberg himself admitted as much when facing Senate hearings in April 2018, where he said he was "open to suggestions" on regulating the Web. The question remains exactly how.

Does AI require a leash?

Artificial intelligence (AI) is another hot candidate for regulation. Elon Musk, the founder of Tesla and other high-tech companies, was right in 2017 when he urged governments around the world to step in and introduce guidelines for AI "before it's too late!" But how do you regulate something if you don't know exactly where it is heading and what its repercussions on society will be?

Generations of sci-fi writers have conjured up nightmare scenarios of superhuman robots running wild and attempting to rule the world. The famous author Isaac Asimov laid out his "Three Laws of Robotics" as far back as 1942 in his *Foundation* trilogy as a sort of code of conduct for intelligent machines:

1. A robot may not injure a human being or, through inaction, allow a human being to come to harm.
2. A robot must obey orders given it by human beings except where such orders would conflict with the First Law.
3. A robot must protect its own existence as long as such protection does not conflict with the First or Second Law.

In 1968, director Stanley Kubrick produced *2001 – Space Odyssey* based on the assumption that Asimov's rules for robots could go horribly wrong. In the film, an invisible, all-seeing robot named Hal misfunctions during an interplanetary flight. When the astronaut tries to shut off and repair the computer, Hal sees its own existence imperiled and kills the human to protect itself (the third rule).

So Asimov apparently needs an update. One was furnished by Oren Etzioni, the director (now CEO) of the Allen Institute for Artificial Intelligence, who wrote an editorial piece for the *New York Times* in 2017 entitled "How to Regulate Artificial Intelligence"; it has been the focus of intense debate ever since.

- First, writes Etzioni, artificial intelligence needs to be subject to the same rules and regulations as mankind. Humans should not be allowed to talk their way out of responsibility by claiming that AI did something they couldn't understand or expect. Should a computer perpetrate a crime such as stock market fraud or a terrorist attack, the owner or operator should be called to account. The same should go for autonomous vehicles in case a pedestrian or a human motorist is injured or killed. Existing loopholes in traffic and other laws need to be filled immediately by authorities or stock market watchdogs.
- Second, AI systems should be obliged to identify themselves so that is clear at all times whether the locutor is a machine or a human being. That way, we could avoid a repeat of the meddling that took place during the

presidential election of 2016 where AI chatbots were employed to call voters, impersonating staffers working for the Trump campaign, as scientists at the University of Cambridge discovered.

- Third, and perhaps most importantly: No artificially intelligent system should be allowed to transmit confidential information without the express consent of the party concerned; the *fons et origo*, so to speak. Cognitive computers such as IBM's Watson are already able to search the entire internet in microseconds and generate insights much faster than any human. The danger, obviously, is that Watson fill find something that was supposed to remain confidential. And what about the sardine-can sized "smart speakers" by Amazon, Google, Microsoft, and Apple that are to be found in growing numbers in our homes, often next to our sofas or beds, and with whom we conduct increasingly sophisticated conversations about everything under the sun – including our most inner secrets. The AI systems behind these "chatbots" have cute names like "Alexa" or "Siri", and they don't just talk – they also listen all the time, even when we have forgotten they're there. And they are capable of transmitting everything they hear to their human masters half-way around the world, providing intimate information that can be recombined with similar secrets from others; in the worst case scenario, the information could be used against us. Imagine the things a child whispers into the ear of a Barbie doll and what an insurance company – or the police – might do based on that information! An autonomous vacuum cleaner could deliver a floorplan of your house to someone just dying to pay a visit when you're not at home. "This is all information we desperately want to keep under our control", says Etzioni.

Self-learning algorithms potentially pose ever greater problems. Who is liable if a self-programming computer comes to certain conclusions without the assistance of any human operator? A self-driving car, for instance, might make life-or-death decisions in dangerous traffic situations, based on its estimate of the future value of the individuals involved; it may run over granny to save the baby in the perambulator since the kid, after all, might be the next Einstein. If the developers of AI systems can wriggle out by claiming that they had no hand in the programming, then society will collapse! AI needs to be made to understand that a human life has absolute value, and there is no way to add or subtract absolutes. Machines must not be allowed to make that kind of decision. That should be the ethical imperative governing all kinds of technology, be they dumb or self-learning.

A New Data Deal

While the Wild West lead directly to the Gilded Age of unconstrained greed capitalism, the period immediately following was marked by a powerful counter-surge of social activism and political reform often referred to as the "Progressive era" and during which the worst excesses of the Industrial Revolution, of urbanization and widespread corruption were reversed and attempts made at reestablishing social justice and common sense. This development in

America coincided with the rise of the Social Democratic movements in Europe, and over the next roughly 30 years encrusted political structures were demolished; the courts went after monopolies, attempts were made to improve working conditions, child labor was abolished and women's suffrage laws were passed. It was time for the "trust busters" to enter the act, beginning with Theodore Roosevelt who oversaw the breakup of Standard Oil to Woodrow Wilson, who championed the eight-hour week for women as well as the establishment of trade unions and cooperatives. The height was reached just before the stock market crash of 1929 and the subsequent Great Depression, the impact of which Franklin Delano Roosevelt worked to alleviate through a series of programs, public work projects, financial reforms and regulations collectively known as the "New Deal".

In his book entitled *Capitalism Included*, Uwe Jean Heuser, a journalist working for the liberal-leaning weekly *Die Zeit*, raised the possibility of a "New Data Deal" which he believes could have a similar positive effect on the digital economy. Data, after all, is the new crude oil driving the business models of Google, Amazon, Facebook, Apple and their ilk, leaving the data owners out in the cold. What do they get in return? he asks. The answer is, of course, nothing, at least up to now. In his article, Heuser explores ways to create a new, fairer and, above all, socially inclusive deal on how our data is used.

The business model GAFA forces us to accept is anything but fair, he believes. "To access a service, we first have to accept the terms and conditions laid down by the service provider which gives him the right to unrestricted commercial use of our data, effectively signing over ownership to Google or whoever. As individuals, we have no choice but to accept – or go without whatever information or service it was we requested." In his opinion, the process first needs to be completely transparent to the user; consumers should be informed of the consequences, the risks and what we get in return so that we can make an informed decision. This kind of transparency would require giving us customers and consumers complete access to the personal data gathered about us by the service provider. Complete access means more than just an extract of the raw data itself, as Facebook does. The way things are handled now, all we get is a statement about how much crude oil we have supplied. The data refineries need to open up and tell what is happening with the petroleum products distilled from it. This should include the right to set limits on what uses the data can be put to. In order to fully realize our personal rights, we should be able to see with whom we are to be seen on photos and who can read our names in the captions, especially if the system has matched us with our personal profiles.

In Germany, the Justice Minister Katarina Barley, a social democrat, demands the creation of open interfaces for all social web services. Open APIs (Application Programming Interfaces) would enable the exchange of data between programs and platforms and would allow individual users to move their data from one service to another, say from WhatsApp to Snapchat or Slack. Open interfaces would make digital life much easier.

In his book *Data for the People*, published in 2017, the former chief scientist of Amazon, Andreas Weigend, lists six basis data rights which would empower people to make better decisions:

- The right to access your data

- The right to inspect data refineries

- The right to amend data

- The right to blur your data

- The right to experiment with different data refineries

- The right to port your data

Both sides—data creators and data companies—stand to benefit from more transparency, Weigend argues. He believes that many efforts to opt out of data tracking and collection are not necessarily in the best interest of the individual. Since we have come to rely on big data services to help us decide which goods and services match our wants and needs, we will need to cooperate with the data companies to help us get from to our desired destination, whether we're looking for a ride across town or a lifelong romantic partner.

In exchange, he says, we need to have tools and mechanisms that allow us to balance the risks, costs and benefits, and be given far greater latitude in deciding exactly with whom we share our data, what for and how much we chose to reveal about ourselves.

Weigend recognizes that we are up against a conundrum here that is caused by geography. The cultures on both sides of the Atlantic are miles apart when it goes to questions of data protection and privacy, but also about the basic role of government in regulating the internet. And then, of course, there are authoritarian or criminal regimes, from Russia to China to Saudi Arabia, who also need to be brought to heel if any major international agreement on these sensitive issues is to succeed, which seems doubtful. All we can hope for, it seems, is that the liberal democracies get together and create a common rulebook that they can impose and enforce. Is this wishful thinking?

Will Europe save the Web?

There is hope. In a dossier for the Washington Post published in May, 2018, authors Tony Romm, Craig Timberg and Michael Birnbaum stated that "Europe, not the US, is now the most powerful regulator of Silicon Valley." Recent developments indicate they may be right.

- In June 2018, the EU commissioner for trade, Margrethe Vestager, announced the largest fine yet against a company, Google, which is being ordered to pay €4.3 billion (about $5 billion) after being convicted of illegally limiting its competitor's access to its smartphone operating system, Android, in order to cement its market leadership position.
- Just weeks earlier the British government fined Facebook £5,000,000 for failing to adequately protect its customers' data and allowing market researchers from Cambridge Analytica to harvest data from 87 million Facebook accounts and use them to create voter profiles, which they subsequently peddled to Donald Trump's election campaign.

- Earlier that year the EU Commission penalized Facebook to the tune of €110 million (about $126 million) for exchanging data with its subsidiary WhatsApp and then lying about it to investigators.
- In 2017, it was Google's turn to pay €2.42 billion (about $2.7 billion) for abusing its search engine's market power to ensure its own ads ranked higher than competitors'.
- Months later, the EU Commission convicted Amazon of accepting illegal tax discounts from Luxembourg and forced them to repay €250 million (about $290 million) in lost revenue.
- Around the same time, the EU Commission decreed that its member state, Ireland, would have to cough up €13 billion (about $15 billion) in back taxes for undercharging Apple over the decades (Ireland has appealed the ruling).

Not only GAFA have learned to fear the EU. Europe, after all, is the second largest economy in the world with some 510 million inhabitants and a domestic product of more than $17 trillion! European cities and countries have been cracking down, for instance, on Uber which was sentenced in Germany and France to pay €800,000 (about $917,000) for going against existing passenger transportation legislation. AirBnB has engaged in catfights with authorities from Barcelona to Berlin because of illegal short-term rentals despite laws in place to prevent shortages of residential space. Apartment owners caught letting tourists stay over face stiff fines.

However, the area causing most controversy is privacy protection, where Europe is starting to show

America who's boss. In May 2014, the European High Court decreed that individuals have the right, under certain conditions, to require search engines to delete links pointing at information about them without first having to prove that the information to be found there is factually wrong. Dubbed "the right to be forgotten", the decision was aimed primarily at newspapers that have become irrelevant or out of date, but which often hang on for years and follow someone for decades. This obligation to delete on request has since been adopted as part of the recently passed European General Data Protection Regulation, or EUGDPR in EU-speak, making it part of the law of the land in all European member states. Web user must also expressly allow companies to store and process their personal data (the so-called "opt-in principle") as opposed to the "opt-out principle" common (and legal) in the United States. In other words, GAFA and others can gather all the data they want about us as long as we don't stand up and forbid them to.

A Viennese GAFA loves to hate

Max Schrems, an Austrian from Salzburg, is probably better known in the US than in his native Europe, and his name is a bugbear for most GAFA executives. A trained lawyer, Schrems has long been in the habit of successfully suing them, the first time in 2015, when the European High Court (EuGH) shredded the so-called Safe Harbor Agreement between the US and Europe, that had allowed European companies and the European subsidiaries of American tech companies to exchange personal data freely if they could demonstrate compliance with the agreement. Schrems proved to the court's satisfaction that the big internet companies like Microsoft's Skype, Google, YouTube, Facebook, Apple, and AOL routinely shared customer data with the US National Security Agency (NSA) – so much for the idea of a "safe" harbor! On October 6, 2015, the EuGH declared the treaty null and void.

In 2014, Schrems tried to launch a class action lawsuit against Facebook which gathered more than 25,000 signatures within weeks. The EuGH refused to hear the case, however, on technical legal grounds. In 2016, Schrems was awarded the Pioneer Award by the Electronic Frontier Foundation, citing his achievements in the field of digital human rights. In late 2017, Schrems founded data protection society he named *noyb* (short for "none of your business"), which seeks to force internet companies to comply with European data protection norms. The society collects donations to finance class action lawsuits against data misuse.

The EUGDPR, despite its unpronounceable name, is sure to change the online world. "Ironically, many Americans are going to find themselves protected from a foreign law. This is not something we are accustomed to", says Rohit Chopra, a member of the Federal Trade Commission (FTC) and its most aggressive privacy regulator. "The path to privacy in the United States has to be fought through Europe," said Jeff Chester, executive director of the Center for Digital Democracy, a privacy watchdog group.

So, will Europe set standards in privacy and data protection for the rest of the world to follow? Ailidh Callander, a spokesman for the British organization Privacy International, believes so. Despite operating branch offices all over Europe (not to mention employing armies of lobbyists in Brussels), US internet companies lack the kind clout that has protected them from government harassment in America, especially under the current administration that would like less intervention in business rather than more.

"Europe is providing a preview of what will eventually happen in the US", says Democratic Senator Edward J. Markey. "Every day that goes by will make more and more people realize that the privacy is under attack. Politicians will have no alternative but to bow to public pressure and put the big internet companies on a leash."

Chapter 4: GAFA must help itself

Technology is morally neutral until we put it to use.

Gerd Leonhard, Futurist

Commons is a word used to describe the cultural and physical resources accessible to all members of a society, resources such as pastures or woodlands in England before most of it was enclosed in the 18th and 19th centuries. Today, the "knowledge commons" is defined as shared resources which enable the distribution and communal ownership of information-nal resources and technology. Instances include open source software like the computer operating system Linux or the free encyclopedia *Wikipedia,* which is based on a model of openly editable content, thus combining the collective intelligence of its users.

If the internet is indeed a cooperative institution, then things like solidarity and partnership become at least as important as connectivity. Robert Metcalfe, an internet pioneer and the inventor the Ethernet, in an essay written in 1980, described what he termed the "network effect". According to Metcalfe, the benefit of a telecommunications network is proportional to the square of the number of connected users. Theodore Vail, the CEO of Bell Telephone, argued back in 1908 that, in the end, a monopoly would benefit customers of long-distance services.

When Alexander Graham Bell's patents on the telephone expired in the mid-1890s, thousands of local telephone companies cropped up, resulting in ridiculous scenarios where the same house might be served by multiple telephones, and where competing companies would deliberately rip up each other's lines in an effort at sabotage. Vail believed a unified, high-quality network could only be achieved if the entire nation's telephone infrastructure was under the control of a single firm. Preferably his own.

As the technology scholar Tim Wu points out in his study of the information industry, *The Master Switch*, running long-distance phone lines exclusively meant being able to combine those operations to create a "powerhouse of distance communications."

Vail summarized his vision with a slogan he introduced in 1908: "One Policy, One System, Universal Service." AT&T, the successor to Bell Telephone, was destined to become an important exception to the rule that monopolies were inherently evil.

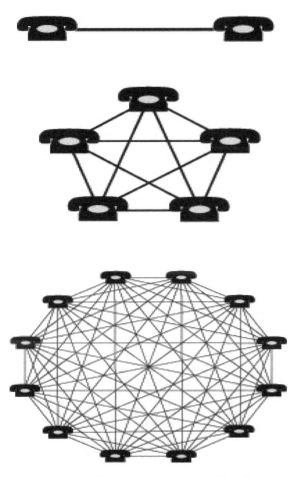

The network effect as demonstrated by the example of a telephone network

The invigorating feeling of setting off on an exciting journey that John Perry Barlow, a cyberlibertarian, songwriter for The Grateful Dead, and the author of *A Declaration of the Independence of Cyberspace* and his many friends shared in the early days of the internet is reflected in the name of the organization they created, the Electronic Frontier Foundation. Barlow envisioned the internet almost as a new nation-state, a digital utopia free from the imperialistic hierarchies and rules of the physical world. He proudly proclaimed that "we are creating a world that all may enter without privilege or prejudice accorded by race, economic power, military force or station of birth" — a place where, he continued, "your legal concepts of property, expression, identity, movement and context do not apply to us. They are all based on matter, and there is no matter here."

Like the early settler crossing the Great Plains they, too, were full of hope and a sense of leaving the old world behind in search of a new one that would transcend the borders of time and space, where there would be justice for all and endless opportunities to spread oneself and live your dreams. And in this world, information would, of course, be free.

Looking back from a world of giant internet monopolies, of data theft and total transparency and, above all, obscene corporate profits, it's hard to imagine just how starry-eyed we were in the early days, when cyberspace looked like the Emerald City and we were all off to the see the wizard. Well, we're not in Kansas anymore, but instead in Silicon Valley, which looks a lot like the Magic Kingdom of Oz in some ways, and where smoke and mirrors are GAFA's tools of choice. And while we weren't watching, the wicked witches took our data, turned them into gold and stashed it away in their castles.

GAFA and others have been helping themselves uninvited to our data for decades now, and they have used it to create wealth for themselves and their stockholders, but for consumers and citizens not so much. What promised to be a machine that would fulfill all our wishes has become the biggest eye in the sky surveillance system no one ever imagined, a

digital panopticon. The anonymity of the net that
Barlow and his friends dreamed of has brought us a
frightening, polarizing climate of flame wars and
shitstorms, of cyber-mobbing and trolls. The free-
flowing exchange of ideas has run up against the wall
of resistance by the so-called creatives, the authors,
the scriptwriters and the filmmakers who see their
business models under threat, who complain about
the loss of social value in art, the decline in status of
artists and the rise of plagiarism – as if plagiarists
were a product of the internet. The online platforms
that were originally designed to bring us closer
together are now driving huge wedges through
society through their misuse as political weapons,
such as by neo-Nazis at home, or by authoritarian
regimes abroad such as Russia or China. John Perry
Barlow, who passed away in February 2018, is surely
spinning in his grave.

Is the internet obsolete?

A less-discussed problem about the internet is that it
is built on ancient technology, at least in digital terms.
My old friend Vinton Cerf, who together with his
fellow student Bob Kahn invented the TCP/IP protocol
way back in 1973, freely admits this. Like dog years, a
year in internet time is supposed to equal seven years
in "real" time, so the basic protocol that runs the
Web is now as if it is over 300 years old and due for
an update. And Vint, whose official title at Google is
now "Elder Statesman" (how I envy him for it!), would
be the first to acknowledge that those were more
innocent times; nobody then foresaw anything like
phishing, spoofing, trolling, electronic harassment,
ransomware, denial of service attacks or the Dark
Web (the Web itself was still a glimmer in Tim

Berners-Lee's eye), much less issues like trust or data integrity. Besides, they were all students, anyway, and they assumed everybody else was a nice person, someone you would love to sit down and hoist a couple of beers with. In fact, in those days, everybody actually *knew* everybody else on the internet and had probably had already had a few with them!

When I last talked to him, Vint acknowledged that some things need fixing, but basically, he believes, TCP/IP has more good sides than bad. Yes, it would be nice if we could somehow build-in security, and it would be nice if we would all switch to IP version 6, since the old version 4 is rapidly running out of addresses (as a 32-bit system it was only has less than 4.3 billion addresses available. In an IoT world where every machine needs its own internet address, the switch to the 128-bit version 6 is crucial to the survival of the Web since it can accommodate approximately 3.4×10^{38} network addresses – that a number with 38 zeroes, so that should be enough to keep the internet running until we're all long gone).

So, if people like Evan Williams, one of Twitter's founders, think "the internet is broken", as he told the *New York Times* in 2017, then what do they mean? Criticism like this usually centers around the basic structure of the internet, which was built on the client/server principle, a distributed system in which software is split between server tasks and client tasks. The analogy here is a customer who sends an order (request) to a vendor (server) who send back goods and an invoice (response). The order form and the invoice form together form the "protocol" used to communicate. When the internet was young, data was generally hosted on powerful mainframe computers (servers), and users logged in via dumb terminals (clients). This gives the owner of the server tremendous power, but for a while in the 1980s and 1990s it looked like the central server was domed; computers became decentralized and thus more democratic. Anyone with a personal computer could host their own data and applications, so who needed servers? Except that as the internet grew, the client/server principle came back into fashion. TCP/IP, seen in this light, was actually a step backwards. It has brought us gigantic server farms and data silos that are only accessible through portals and platforms controlled by – you guessed! – Google, Amazon, Facebook, and Apple, along with a handful of other data titans and app providers, all out to gather as much of our personal data as they possibly can to store on their servers and then monetize in one way or another.

Dirk Trossen, a senior principal scientist at *InterDigital*, a networking consultancy based in Delaware, is convinced that, on the internet at least, we've hit the end of the road for clients and servers. "The client-server paradigm made a lot of sense when the internet started out because, in those days, information was scarce. It was usually locked somewhere. It lived behind a 'portal'," he told *Wired* magazine in December 2017. A portal, as he describes it, is like a door we have to knock on to get entry, for instance to a big library. But today, information lives everywhere so the idea of having to go somewhere to get it seems old-fashioned in the extreme.

Can pirate software save the Web?

Trossen and his friends are trying to create an "information-centric network" (ICN), an internet that is independent of geography – just like Barrow imagined at the very beginning of the World Wide Web. Instead of URLs (uniform resource locators) –

the web addresses used today to access servers and information - an ICN-based internet would use URIs (uniform resource identifiers). Imagine them as tiny labels affixed to a bunch of data to tell everyone else what kind of information it contains. To access the information, it would be enough to send out a call through the Web and let the network find out where it is and retrieve it for us.

An ICN-based internet would be much faster than ours today. It turns out, namely, that ICN uses a technology that is a favorite of video pirates, BitTorrent, a collaborative file sharing protocol that is perfect for sharing large amounts of data quickly. Instead of sending requests and results back and forth as client/server systems do, BitTorrent creates a separate distribution network for each individual file. These files can exist simultaneously in hundreds or even thousands of copies at various points around the globe – on disk drives or smartphones of people who downloaded the file at some time in the past.

BitTorrent can even retrieve bits and pieces of a file from different locations and fit them together, which drastically shortens the so-called "latency" of the system, namely the time it needs to download the desired file. For instance, the system could download a single copy of a Netflix or YouTube video to multiple users at the same time, only slightly time-delayed. This would also reduce transmission costs.

ICN could also potentially solve the biggest problem the internet has today, namely lack of trust. Since each data packet can be positively identified through its URI, it can be easily traced back to its point of origin. Instantly, things like pirating, phishing, or fake news would be a thing of the past! Nowadays, criminals identify themselves as good guys through a technique called IP spoofing that tricks the addressee into believing that the data is coming from a trusted host. Taking over a website, a browser or an entire network is easy this way, which is why it is the favorite method for most cybercrooks. The trick is to persuade users to connect to a different server than the one they think they are accessing. Since servers are irrelevant in an ICN network, and because the information itself is identifiable, this backdoor is blocked. The URI can even be programmed to include information about the user who is authorized to see it, so nobody else gets to peek!

Where pathways cross in cyberspace, a node is created. If lots of pathways meet, we call them supernodes. Perhaps the best example is Facebook with its 2 billion+ users – about two thirds of the earth's inhabitants. This huge online population is constantly generating loads and loads of data that Facebook is able to turn into profits - $9 billion per quarter in 2019 alone!

One of the best-known detractors of supernodes is Aral Balkan, and activist, web designer and the developer of Ind.ie, a small activist group in Malmö, Sweden, that agitates for more social justice in digital society.

Balkan has developed a piece of software called Better Blocker that protects the privacy of people using Apple's Safari web browser. Today, online advertisers use a host of tools to monitor users' web behaviors, what they buy and where they are located. Called "geotracking", this system works just as well on PCs as on smartphones. One such tool are web bugs, also known as web beacons or tracking pixels – invisible dots inserted into a website or an e-mail that are capable of sending back information about users such as their IP addresses, the website they are visiting, the time and type of browser and more – even if the user hasn't clicked on anything! If we are lucky, all that this leads to is our being targeted by the advertiser to get more of the same kind of ads; in the worst case, hackers can use the information to infiltrate our systems and do mischief.

Balkan wants to break the power of the supernodes by giving users their very own node – a tiny piece of the internet where they can control their private data and decide themselves who gets to see or use their information. Such a system would be completely decentralized, so data would no longer have to flow through a supernode. Instead, we could, for instance, send a photo to a friend directly, since all user nodes are connected to one another.

Ethics incorporated

Underlying his vision of a decentralized internet is something Balkan calls "ethical design". For him, this means a technology that respects users' basic human rights, for instance, their right of informational self-determination or the right to be forgotten. Ethical design, he believes should provide a positive experience through an intuitive and unobtrusive interface. "Technology belongs in the background of our lives", he believes. "It gives you joy. It empowers you with superpowers. It puts a smile on your face and makes your life better."

Balkan is by no means the only one working on a decentralized version of the internet. Tim Berners-Lee, the inventor of the World Wide Web who now works at MIT, recently announced an initiative he called *Solid*, a name derived from the phrase "social linked data". He wants to create conventions and tools that will provide decentralized social applications through a system of networked data. Like ICM, Solid works with Uniform Resource Locators (URIs) which link individual bits of information directly. Another contestant in the race to decentralization is the Mozilla Foundation, that recently announced a $2 million prize for the best ideas in this field. Name.com, an accredited domain name registrar and web hosting company based in Denver, Colorado, wants to use blockchain technology to forge direct, trustworthy links between information and its users. Users will be able to identify themselves through a kind of digital ID card called Namecoin Identities, which will enable users to prove they really are who they say they are. In New York, a company called Monegraph is already using Namecoin to link Twitter accounts to digital assets – a text, a picture, a video – so that the owner of the asset can track who has downloaded something, whether he or she has paid for it and what they do with it later, such as loan it to a friend or sell it on to someone else.

Resistance from within

This is a bad time to work for a Silicon Valley company. Be it Google or Facebook, employees are beginning to feel the social pressure from without. Big tech companies are being compared to Big Tobacco; Congress has gotten in the habit of hauling tech CEOs before hearings where they have to answer tough questions about their company's behavior and business models. Increasingly, they are being accused of undermining liberal democracies, poisoning the brains of children and censoring information. No, earning your bread in Silicon Valley sure ain't as pleasant as it used to be, even if the pay is still good.

Tech workers are often oversensitive, and this kind of talk is demotivating. In fact, the staff of some GAFA companies are themselves raising the hue and cry against their employers' lack of social responsibility. Employees of Google, Facebook, Intel and Cisco recently gathered at the Palo Alto headquarters of Palantir, a company specializing in Big Data analysis, to protest the announcement that the company would be supplying immigration authorities with the means to create a citizen database that could be used against followers of Islam in the United States. Palantir's CEO is known as a staunch supporter of Donald Trump and his plans to deport thousands of people from Muslim countries. "Being forced to collaborate with the US government on large-scale human rights abuses is the first time I've ever seen that made high-end tech workers unionize," said Valerie Aurora, one of the protestors and the founder of Frame Shift, a consulting firm training startups on inclusion and diversity. A couple of week later, 3,000 Google workers signed a letter protesting the announcement that the search engine giant had agreed to develop an AI system to improve the accuracy of the weapons systems on combat drones.

Now wouldn't it just be ironic if the same companies that gave us data theft, digital heteronomy, fake news, hate postings, information overload and total transparency were forced by their own people to rethink and mend their ways? After all, nobody believes these companies couldn't turn their power of innovation into finding technical solutions for many of the problems they have themselves created.

"There are few signs that Washington is capable of policing the use of emerging technologies", writes tech correspondent Kevin Roose in the *New York Times*. "And while companies like Google have formed their own AI ethics groups, those groups are ultimately powerless if executives decide to ignore their advice." That may be the big opportunity for tech workers to unionize (something they have been reluctant to do previously). But even if they don't, there are already plenty of pressure groups springing up all around the Valley. The Tech Workers Coalition, for instance, is a group of hundreds of concerned industry employees with chapters in San Francisco, Seattle and San Jose. Another group called Tech Action has been active in New York since last year. The Center for Humane Technology, also made up of former tech employees, has gone public with demands for ethical product development. Flush with money from a $7 million donation, the CHT boasts Google's former head of "design ethics" Tristan Harris; as well as Roger McNamee, one of Mark Zuckerberg's former advisors; Lynn Fox, the former head of PR at Apple and Twitter; as well as Justin Rosenstein, the guy who invented the "like" button for Facebook, among its founding members.

"Our society is being hijacked by technology", the group says on its homepage, www.humantech.com. "What began as a race to monetize our attention is now eroding the pillars of our society: mental health, democracy, social relationships, and our children. They are part of a system designed to addict us."

Are algorithms racist?
The easiest way to fix the internet would be to focus the enormous power of artificial intelligence, which GAFA is so keen to develop and promote, on finding solutions for everything from cyber-mobbing to kiddie porn, hate speak, and fake news. Surely the right kind of algorithm should be capable of dealing

with things that are either offensive, immoral or politically incorrect. A simple mouse click, and they would go away. Or wouldn't they?

Unfortunately, things are not that simple. First, we would have to agree on what is offensive, immoral or politically incorrect. Fat chance of that happening! *Autres pays, autre merde*, as the French say. Or, if that sounds too offensive for you: Other countries, other manners.

Whose feelings should we respect, then? In 1998, Microsoft introduced its first-generation search engine, MSN Search, and then-CEO Steve Ballmer travelled to Munich to host a press conference about it, which I attended. Of course, Microsoft wouldn't allow anything smutty or illegal to appear on their search results, Steve insisted. When asked how to define "smutty", we hemmed and hawed and finally came out with the riposte: "nudity and sex".

Some journalists pointed out to him that Europeans tend to have a more laid-back attitude towards nudity and matters sexual than do puritan Americans. Europeans, on the other hand, strongly disapprove, as a rule, of graphic scenes of violence, which are staple fare for movies and videos produced in the US. In fact, many overseas productions are banned by the European authorities from being shown to kids.

Finally, driven into a corner by the barrage of questions as to whose standards Microsoft would follow, he blurted out: "Well, ours, of course!"

Conceivably, the large internet corporations would need to develop blocking algorithms for each individual country. And anyway, we still have time to think this over. AI, it turns out, isn't as smart yet as their creators would like us to believe.

In 2015, Google caused a big scandal when it turned out that its new neuronal picture-recognition system was identifying black people as gorillas. Which immediately posed the question: Can algorithms be racist?

Computer scientists have been aware of the problem now for quite a while. They call the phenomenon "bias by data", meaning prejudice that is determined by the choice of data. In this case, Google's developers had neglected to show its algorithm pictures of black people during its training, so having only ever seen humans with white skin, it concluded that these must be some totally different animal, and gorillas seemed to be the closest match.

Sexist bots, racist AI: "That algorithms are somehow neutral by nature is a myth", says Klaas Wilhelm Bollhoefer, founder and Managing Director of Birds on Mars, an IT company based in Berlin. Machines are just as incapable of objective analysis as humans. "The idea of somehow being able to reach objective decisions automatically belong to legend, and we should keep it there", be believes.

Recently, the number of cases in which filter mechanisms fail has been growing. In 2017, counterfeit episodes of the children's cartoon series *PAW Patrol* started cropping up on *YouTube Kids*. Some of the figures wound up committing suicide or being beset by demons. In other episodes, some of the figures urinated on each other. Worried parents flooded YouTube with complaints. A company spokesman claimed that cases such as these were "the extreme needle in the haystack", given that YouTube viewers upload 400 hours of video each minute and are watching more than one billion hours of video a day, but was forced in the end to admit that the filter algorithm had somehow misfunctioned.

Often, they fail altogether. Alice Marwick from Data & Society, a research lab financed in part by Microsoft, claims that the prevailing cultural mindset in Silicon Valley is to blame. None dares to address the subject, she says, because "everybody is scared to death of being nailed to the cross by internet censors and industry watchdogs." Tech firms, she believes, are like the three Indian monkeys of legend, whose motto was "speak no evil, hear no evil, see no evil."

The only way to force the tech companies to respond is to apply the thumbscrew. John Adams, the former lead security engineer at Twitter, suggested in an interview in *Fast Company* that venture capitalists could demand a "harassment strategy" before funding a project. Others have suggested generous bonuses for employees who successfully develop anti-abuse software – just like some companies pay hackers to penetrate their corporate defenses to show them where the vulnerabilities are. All of this will require full support from top management, so don't expect things to get moving anytime soon. If your primary focus is on earning as much money as you possibly can, investing in intelligent filter systems probably won't be your greatest priority.

Such systems wouldn't be impossible – just impossibly expensive in the eyes of senior management. Take Facebook, for instance: Since 2016 the company has faced a barrage of criticism for standing by as Russian operatives created thousands of manipulated accounts churning out fake news about the Democratic candidate during the last presidential election, almost certainly throwing the race to Trump.

Mark Zuckerberg never ceases to declaim that
"protecting our society is more important than
maximizing profits". The last time he said that was
before the Senate panel investigating him and his
company, and later the same day he complained to
reporters that Facebook's operating costs would rise
by "45 to 60%" if it were forced to introduce
artificially intelligent filter systems and human
firefighters, a.k.a. "content managers". (More about
these unfortunate individuals in a minute under
"digital sin eaters".)

So, it all boils down to a matter of conscience for
Facebook and the others. What is more important –
being trusted or earning lots of money? The answer
isn't as straightforward as it may seem. Loss of
trustworthiness can impact a company's bottom line
as well as its stock market performance. At the end of
the day, Facebook will have to shell out for intelligent
filters for news and ads if it doesn't want to see
young users especially leaving in droves to move to
other social web applications they deem more
principled. After all, there are enough of them
around. And remember the sad fate of MySpace –
here today, gone tomorrow!

It's a global problem: If people in developing
countries grow up believing that big internet
companies are dishonest and undependable, the
more it will cost them to change their image. And of
course, those companies that chose to invest in
credibility will grow, while others will fall behind.
That's called free market economy, and social
acceptance and public trust are just as important as
transformational products and marketing prowess.

Plus, there is the danger of humanity as a whole
falling into what Nicholas Negroponte, the former

head of the MIT Media Lab, once called the "digital divide". He used it to describe a "world of information-haves and information have-nots", and he worried that tech-savvy industrialized nations would pull far ahead of poor, digitally deprived countries whose population would lack basic digital skills and access to the technologies such as the internet. When I talked with him in 2015, he was keen on making "digital inclusion" a watchword and a major political goal.

By now, of course, almost everybody on the planet is connected to the World Wide Web, although often in a limited or tightly censored form. If trust is not established by the big internet companies, a new digital divide could appear between among people and societies, nations and regions where it is lacking. In authoritarian societies, this lack of trustworthiness could even be abused as an excuse for even more draconian measures to restrict online freedom – disguised as consumer protection or civil rights. And that would be the biggest irony of all!

Digital sin-eaters

As long as the internet giants refuse to develop effective intelligent filters, humans will need to do the dirty jobs. And once more, an analogy with the Wild West thrust itself forward. Early settlers from England brought with them an ancient tradition, namely "sin eating". When a rich man passed away, it was the custom in many rural areas for the family to call for the most miserable man in town, the sin eater. They would place a piece of gold piece on the deceased's chest along with a slice of stale bread which the sin eater would grab and rapidly devour before the mourners chased him out of the house, pelting him all the time with stones or lumps of wood.

Sin eaters fulfilled an important social and religious function by taking upon themselves the sins of the dead whose road to heaven was thereby cleared. While the custom largely died out in England by the end of the 19th century, it persisted in remote areas of the American West for much longer. Reports of sin eaters can be found long into the 20th century in isolated Appalachian valleys and in the Midwest – except no one wanted to talk about it!

Modern sin eaters are called content managers. Like their predecessors, their job is to take our sins upon themselves by spending endless hours watching the worse filth and depravity to which humans are capable, and which regularly crop up on social websites. Every major internet company employs armies of content managers, who are generally poorly paid and considered the lowest of the low by their colleagues and bosses.

In the Berlin suburb of Charlottenburg, more than a thousand men and women employed by Arvato, a subsidiary of the media company Bertelsmann, work in an unassuming converted factory building to rid Facebook of the worst hate postings, kiddie porn, and fake news. All day long, they gaze into the depths of human nature. "The first time I watched a beheading I cried", one young woman told a reporter from *Der Spiegel*. Later, she became jaded. Bertelsmann employs both a full-time psychologist and a social worker. "It's like treating someone with CSR", one of them said – referring to post combat stress reaction, or "combat fatigue" found among GIs returning from Afghanistan.

"We're the dumpster drivers of the internet", one young man told reporters. "They need us – but they despise us."

Facebook refuses to talk about it, but it would appear that the choice of Berlin for their content management center is because of Germany's stringent laws against digital indecency. The *Network Enforcement Act* ("Netzwerkdurchsetzungsgesetz") passed in October 2017 by the former coalition government is often called the "hate speech law" and is applicable to both German and non-German social networks to which Germans may register. It requires operators to delete content that is "manifestly illegal" (such as child rape or homicide), by which is meant that it "can be detected within 24 hours, for instance by trained personnel." The procedure is meant to ensure that the social network provider will take *immediate* note of a complaint and check whether the content in question is unlawful and subject to removal or blocking.

Unlike "manifestly" unlawful content, postings that are simply illegal because they oppose the provisions of the German Criminal Code or constitute offenses against the democratic constitutional state, the public order or the personal honor or sexual self-determination of an individual must also be removed, but the process can take a bit longer. Intentionally spreading fake news can also be considered unlawful content. For instance, a woman in Bavaria spread a rumor on Facebook that a 17-year-old German girl had been molested by foreign immigrants at a refugee center in the small town of Mühldorf. The girl was so badly hurt that she had to undergo emergency surgery, the woman claimed. The whole thing proved to be completely made-up, and the woman was arrested and sentenced to jail for feigning a crime, but by then the false report had already gone viral. It was shared more than 140 times within 13 hours, and it still crops up occasionally on Facebook and other social websites. Fake news is like a hydra, the monster with nine heads in Greek mythology; every time Heracles cut off one of its heads, two more would emerge from the wound.

Besides, one person's fake news it the other one's expression of opinion, and courts in the US are famous for their breadth in interpreting the First Amendment right to free speech. In Europe, they are prone to making short process of anyone's claim that hurtful or damaging language on the Web is just a matter of opinion.

And anyway, just because something is illegal doesn't mean anyone will do something about it. Facebook stands accused of taking its time handling reports of hate-speak or obscene language. Between June 2016 and February 2017, the German Interior Ministry monitored reports submitted to social websites and checked how many of them had been deleted. The result for Facebook: only 39%. For Twitter, only 1%!

It's like the day back in the Wild West, where the sheriff first had to catch a desperado before he could hang him.

Chapter5: We are the Web!

"Democracy is the
worst form of government,
except for all those other forms that have
been tried from time to time."

Winston S. Churchill

Solidarity and society

If Westerners didn't like something, they got together and did something about it. Who else could they turn to? The long arm of the law consisted of a sheriff, who probably lived miles away in the next big town, or the federal marshal, who only came by occasionally. If you happened to live in the lonesome prairie or in some remote valley in the Rockies, you were on your own.

In the days of the Wild West, settlers stuck together and helped each other out. Their only chance of survival against an Indian attack was to circle their wagons. And when a farmer wanted a new outbuilding, he invited the neighbor over for a "barn raising". By nightfall, the new structure was ready, and folks could gather round and start raising Cain! Solidarity and society were much more than abstract terms in those days.

In the wilds of the Web, these values have largely been forgotten. Instead, we sit around trapped in our filter bubbles, lonesome digital egocentrics because the social Web satisfies most of our cravings for approval and self-recognition. It's the only place we can be sure that someone is listening to us.

"What began as a race to monetize our attention is now eroding the pillars of our society: mental health, democracy, social relationships, and our children", says *Humantech.com*, a digital rights organization founded by former GAFA employees and tech investors. (see previous chapter). Its aim is to establish a system of "humane design" as the foundation of a long-overdue "cultural awakening". It also provides the tools consumers and citizens will need if they want to regain control over their lives, change their habits and refine what they want from technology. The first step? Solidarity and society!

Unfortunately, what's best for capturing our attention isn't best for our well-being, according to Humantech. Snapchat turns conversations into streaks, redefining how our children measure friendship. Instagram glorifies the picture-perfect life, eroding our self-worth. Facebook segregates us into echo chambers, fragmenting our communities. YouTube autoplays the next video within seconds, even if it eats into our sleep. "These are not neutral products – they are part of a system designed to addict us", the site warns.

Sociologists have been cautioning for decades about the addictive effects of technologies from television to the internet. The "always on" Web and smartphones raise the level of obsession by several notches. Jonathan Taplin, director emeritus of the University of Southern California's Annenberg Innovation Lab and author of *Move Fast and Break Things – How Facebook, Google, and Amazon Cornered Culture and Undermined Democracy*, wrote: "Google doesn't want what's best for us," in an opinion piece for the *New York Times* in 2017. "The effects of the darker side of tech culture reach well beyond the Valley. It starts with an unwillingness to control fake news and pervasive sexism that no doubt contributes to the gender pay gap."

The question rose to the fore in 2017 when Google fired engineer James Damore for writing a memo that questioned the company's gender-diversity policies and made statements about women's biological unsuitability for technical jobs. In 2014, Google began to promote and encourage diversity after it reluctantly admitted only 17 percent of its technical workforce was female.

Taplin believes that the "bro" culture, which is rampant in Silicon Valley, is at fault, along with the "greed is good" attitude of the large internet companies that rake in record profits every quarter, but fob off their users with a few addictive apps and more or less feckless functions. "We know we are being driven by men like Peter Thiel and Jeff Bezos toward a future that will be better for them. We are not sure that it will be better for us", he believes. "By giving networks like Google and Facebook control of the present, we cede our freedom to choose our future."

Why do we, the "netizens" of the world, always have the sneaky feeling that we are alone and that nobody cares what we think about our own futures?

Its high time we did something about it!

Futurist Gerd Leonhard talks about the concept of digital obesity in his latest book, *Technology vs. Humanity*, which he says is "rapidly developing into a pandemic of unprecedented proportions". He defines this as a mental and technological condition in which data, information, media and general digital connectedness accumulate to such an extent that they begin to have a harmful effect on our health, sense of well-being, and life in general. It's analogous to the way governments around the globe pay lip-service to efforts by the World Health Organization (WHO) to combat the "obesity epidemic" by implementing stronger regulation of the food industry. Despite this, the industry continues to load their products with chemicals for maximum "mouth feel" and "repeat appeal" (addictiveness).

Ironically, most of the world's food giants, faced with complaints of how their products affect our waistlines, have turned around to begin making money from obesity by buying into the diet industry. Taking a page out of the big food companies' book, tech companies today are busy selling us health products like Fitbit trackers or slimming apps. *Calm*, which was named as Apple's App of the Year in 2017, is billed as a meditation and relaxation aid. The San Francisco-based startup offers its users soothing music and guided meditations at a price tag of $60 a year. In March 2018, CNBC reported that Calm's stock market valuation had reached $250m.

Digital fasting

Way back in the good old days of 2010, I wrote a blog post entitled *Digital Fasting* which has lost none of its original relevance:

> *The solution to our problem of digital gluttony is simple: digital fasting! Let's forgo surfing the Web, writing emails and posting on our blogs, at least for a couple of weeks a year. Presto! No more cognitive dissonance, no more social alienation. Our battered brains will be able to recuperate – ingenious!*

> *Okay, there are a few problems we need to solve first. Our work would get stuck, our friends would be upset because we no longer answer their mails, customers will complain to the boss because the stuff they ordered hasn't been delivered. But that will sort itself out.*

> *Devout Catholics fast for 40 days from Ash Wednesday until Easter; seven long weeks without meat. Orthodox Christians distinguish between three kinds of fasting: Strict Fasting means sticking to a vegetarian diet; the only animal product you're allowed to eat is honey; Light Fasting allows you to drink wine and eat oil and seafood; and Fish Fasting lets you eat as much fish as you want.*

> *The online film producer Kirby Ferguson has come up with something he calls the Slow Media Diet. The problem isn't technology, he believes, it's velocity. The solution, he says, is to slow down. For him, audio podcasts are okay but stick away from RSS feeds.*

Abstention has changed his whole life, he maintains: "When I abandoned Twitter I hardly noticed it. And I have become pickier in choosing which websites and blogs to visit; instead I invest my time more wisely in things that really matter".

"Know thyself", the ancient Greeks counseled. But before we can adjust and shake off the bonds of GAFA, we first have to be aware of the harm they are causing. The rest is simply a question of willpower and of solidarity and society. Together, we might just pull through...

Moore's legacy

More than any other functional principle, Moore's Law has changed the world out of all recognition. Gordon Moore, one of the founders of Intel, was only 37 when he recognized that the number of transistors you could pack onto a standard computer chip continued to double every 18 to 24 months. Nothing has changed since, and Moore's Law is firmly enshrined as one of the most gifted perceptions of the Digital Age.

Doubling, as we all know, leads to exponential growth, also known as geometric progression. Leonhard describes it thus: "First very slowly, then very fast!" The step from 1 to 2 and from 2 to 4 may seem like a snail's pace, but when you get up to 16, 32, 64, 128 and above, things start happening with lightning speed.

The best story about exponential growth comes to us from India, where an emperor named Sharan wanted to reward the mathematician who had invented the game of chess and promised to grant him any wish.

The man said he had only a tiny wish. All he wanted was a single grain of rice on the first square of his chess board, two on the second, four on the third, and so on.

Amazed at such modesty, the emperor immediately granted the gift. However, the court treasurer worked out that on the 64th square he would need to deliver 18,446,744,073,709,551,615 grains of rice – a heap larger than Mount Everest and more than 1,000 times the world's annual production of rice. Unfortunately for him, the inventor was beheaded by the ungrateful monarch – but not before he made the point that exponential growth rapidly leads to results we humans can hardly comprehend.

There still seems to be no end in sight for Moore's Law. In 2017, IBM announced that their scientists had managed to pack 30 billion transistors into a computer chip the size of a fingernail.

Or is there perhaps a limit somewhere? "Moore's Law is running out of steam," *The Economist* claimed in 2016. While that may one day be true for semiconductors, it most certainly isn't for technology in general. Besides, in areas such as artificial intelligence and self-learning algorithms, we are still at square one. And remember the tale of the grains of rice: First very slowly, then very fast…

We are rapidly approaching the point where computers will be as powerful as the human brain. Computerologists describe this as the "singularity" and love to speculate about when it will come to pass. "By 2024 at the latest," says Ray Kurzweil, a tech visionary and one of the founders of the Singularity University in Mountain View, California – right in the heart of Silicon Valley. This doesn't mean that computers will be as smart as humans, but their processing power and their ability to deal with complex problems will equal and then very quickly surpass ours. In a year, they will be twice as powerful, in two years four times as powerful, and in three years eight times, and so on – get it?

Computers don't need to seek power – we will hand it over to them

The biggest danger exponential technology poses is that we will become overburdened. Mankind has a long history of passing on its more arduous tasks to machines, starting with the plow and leading, in our time, to robotic lawnmowers and vacuum cleaners. We tend to delegate important decisions to our mechanical helpmates just because they're there and we can.

Take the sat-nav, for instance. The minute we turn one of those gadgets on, we simultaneously switch off our brains and blindly follow the directions given to us – no matter where we end up. Too often, this means getting stuck in a wrong-way street or even in some swamp or bog. In a search for sat-nav blunders Google turned up thousands of results, including an item in the Daily Telegraph stating that "Sat-nav blunders have caused up to 300,000 accidents" in Britain alone. Town councils in England and Wales started setting up road signs as early as 2007 warning truck drivers of narrow thoroughfares where they might get stuck if they trust their digital advisors. Traffic engineers say over-reliance on technology has become a major hazard.

Leonhard fears that humanity will eventually lose control of technology, not because robots are reaching for power but because we are giving it up. He calls this "self-abdication".

Machines, lacking consciousness, don't think and probably never will. But, if we let them, they will make our decisions for us in a growing number of increasingly vital areas. Sooner or later, humans will no longer be able to understand how our machines reach certain conclusions; we will have, in effect, abdicated our self-determination.

In his 19th century novel *The Time Machine*, H G Wells describes a distant future in which the surface of the earth is populated by a race of small, elegant, childlike human beings called Eloi that live happy and carefree lives subsiding on fruit that grows in perfusion, all other needs being supplied by machines. Eventually, the time traveler in the book discovers that there is another race of ape-like troglodytes who live in darkness underground and surface only at night, the Morlocks. These creatures keep the machines running smoothly and in return capture and eat the Eloi. Mankind, it turns out, has evolved over time into two species: the Eloi are the descendants of the leisured classes, the brutal Morlocks are the progeny of the downtrodden laboring classes.

Guy Fawkes send his greetings!

There are already indications that users and consumers are beginning to rethink their relationship with the tech companies in a big way. After two decades of often euphoric delight and approval as well as a willingness to rely increasingly on our gadgets, trust in technology is eroding, at least in the Western world, says Bhaskar Chakravorti of Tuft

University, who led a study in 2018 that turned up a growing wave of digital distrust directed especially at the GAFA companies.

As digital skepticism becomes more widespread, it could conceivably lead to a countercurrent I would like to describe as "digital solidarity". If everyone is angry, they can get together like the barn builders of the Wild West and do something – like increasing the pressure on the tech industry as well as on politicians. Shitstorms, after all, are nothing but the expression of shared frustration and furor, and they have proven capable in the past of bringing down company mail servers and causing computer systems to crash.

Back in the Wild West, angry citizens sometimes banded together and became vigilantes; a word borrowed from Spanish where it means "watchman". The term digital vigilante, or DV for short, has been in use at least since the 1990s and describes people who use the internet as a weapon against those perceived to offend against custom and decency; effectively taking the law into their own hands.

DVs are driven by a variety of motivations including political, economic or moral grounds. For example, the Perverted Justice Foundation in America has waged an unrelenting war against pedophiles by outing police suspects, whether they have been found guilty by a court of justice or not. A sister organization in Britain, called Letzgo Hunting, recently accused a young software engineer named Gary Cleary of posting nude photos of small children online, which drove him to commit suicide. A spokesman for the local police force deplored this use of "amateur methods" which could possibly hamper criminal investigations and destroy the lives of innocent people. At worst, the true perpetrators might take warning, leading them to threaten or even kill the children involved in order to protect themselves.

Many DVs have a political background, such as a group of Chinese hackers who took down the computer systems at CNN, a move they justified as a protest against the broadcaster's coverage of the anti-Chinese independence movement in Tibet.

Sooner or later, DVs will almost certainly turn their attention to GAFA and others, and they will use the weapons supplied to them by these selfsame companies. Launching a sophisticated Distributed Denial-of-Service attack (DDoS), flooding the victims' computers and forcing them to shut down, is as easy as downloading some software from sites like LOIC (Low Orbit Ion Cannon) or HULK (HTTP Unbearable Load King) and following a few simple instructions. "Any eighth-grader can do it", says Pavitra Shankdhar of the Infosec Institute in Elmwood Park, Illinois, a company specializing in enterprise security training.

LOIC is the digital equivalent of an intercontinental ballistic missile and the favorite tool of Anonymous, a self-named online collective of activists that has been blamed for a slew of radical actions and attacks against various organizations, government agencies and large tech concerns. It began as a kind of wacky digital funathon, with online activists joining the Blockupy anti-austerity protests in 2011, wearing Guy Fawkes masks commemorating the Catholic rebel who planned the failed Gunpowder Plot against the English government in 1605. Anonymous directed their first really large-scale cyber-attack against the Church of Scientology, followed by a whole series of incursions of victims such as Sony, ISIS, the German performing rights organization GEMA, and the Egyptian government.

A threatened attack on Facebook, attributed to Anonymous in 2011, proved to be a false alarm but others have followed with similar threats. A group calling itself DadaDada has called on internet users to "free yourselves from Google, Amazon, Facebook and Apple". The group offers a slightly weird app on its homepage that replaces advertising with truly dadaesque images and music. The French software company Framasoft, whose motto is *Dégooglison* (the de-Google-ifying of the internet), offers a range of alternative products to Google's such as Framapad which is supposed to replace Google Docs. Diaspora, billed as a Facebook killer, claims to create "a social online world where you have control over your own data". Users can set links to their existing social Web accounts such as Facebook or Twitter and access them from without, so to speak.

Activists like Anonymous are often grouped with terrorists but one person's terrorist is, of course, another person's freedom fighter; it all depends on who wins in the end. Most people on this planet are peaceful by nature and reluctant to chuck bombs, be those real or merely digital ones. For these people we need to come up with some new ideas.

Helping us to help ourselves

CeBIT, the world's largest IT trade show held each year in Hannover, chose the title Shareconomy for the 2013 expo which has since become a buzzword. The blend word of share and economy describes an economic model based on acquiring, providing or sharing access to goods and services through a community-based online platform. It is also sometimes referred to as collaborative consumption or peer economy. Widespread use of information technologies such as social media and electronic marketplaces, it was assumed, would eventually engender direct interaction between users and organizations as well as increased co-operation and collaboration in all spheres of life.

In his book *The Zero Marginal Cost Society,* published in 2016, the American sociologist Jeremy Rifkin describes how the emerging Internet of Things is speeding us to an era of nearly free goods and services, precipitating the meteoric rise of a global Collaborative Commons and the eclipse of capitalism. Prosumers – people who produce the things they consume – would share their own information, entertainment, green energy, and 3D-printed goods at near zero marginal cost, as well as enrolling in massive open online courses based on the Collaborative Commons. Co-operatives, Rifkin believes, will eventually become the only viable business model and lead to the Fourth Industrial Revolution.

While writing his book, maybe Rifkin was thinking about the Granger movement in the American West during the 19th century. The faction was founded in 1867 by Oliver Hudson Kelley, a former farmer from Minnesota, as a coalition of US farmers called the National Grange of the Patrons of Husbandry. Its purpose was to benefit farm society by reducing isolation, addressing their economic needs and advancing new methods of agriculture.

In the period following the Civil War (1861-1865), the United States went through a period of severe economic depression. About this time, the railroad companies gained a monopoly on grain elevators, a fast new system for loading grain onto railroad cars for transportation to the distant markets in the Eastern states. Also known as Prairie Skyscrapers, the elevators made the farmers feel victimized by the exorbitant freight rates they were forced to pay to the so-called railroad barons. Since the movement and storage of grain were considered to be closely related to public interest, pressure grew to put a stop to these practices, and in 1887, Congress passed the Interstate Commerce Act banning "any conspiracy in restraint of trade". It was the first anti-trust law passed in America and an important precursor to the Sherman Act of 1890. The new act established a completely new legal principle called "reasonable and just", which implies that businesses have a duty to act in good faith and deal fairly – a truly novel idea at the time (and again today?).

Co-operatives are up-to-date for another reason, too, because another way of looking at them is as a customer-centric relationship network in which many vendors choose to work together in the interest of the customer. A good example is Autobytel, which changed its name to AutoWeb in 2017 after acquiring the pay-per-click automobile advertising network of that name. The company succeeded in becoming one of the leading car dealerships in the US – which is ironic because AutoWeb does not actually sell cars. In fact, it is a new breed of company, sometimes referred to as an "infomediary", whose role in life is to create a network of vendors and service providers, each capable of fulfilling part of the needs of a customer interested in purchasing a car or motorbike: dealerships (cars), carmakers (info about types and models), garages (spare parts, maintenance), banks (financing), and insurers (coverage) each provide a part of the puzzle that in the end surrounds customers so tightly that to leave and go elsewhere would leave them worse off. Finally, AutoWeb links to all major social Web platforms where customers can exchange experiences and give each other helpful tips.

In a way, AutoWeb has created a digital co-operative; one that is maintained by all of the participating companies themselves. This is sometimes referred to as co-opetition, namely when competitors band together because it is in the best interest of all their customers.

Customer-centric relationship networks

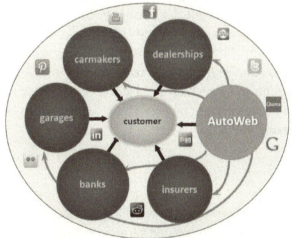

The only real problem with digital co-ops is that they are mostly short-lived. They are formed spontaneously on the Web when a certain special need arises and disband again once that need has been satisfied. The National Cooperative Business Association (NCBA) in the US has a membership of more than 29,000 co-operative businesses employing more than two million people and accounting for over $650bn in annual revenue. These businesses reach from such august associations as the Associated Press (AP) to the National Credit Union Foundation, from the National Football League (NFL) to the Capitol Hill Babysitting Co-op. There was even an Amazon Bookstore Cooperative which initially had nothing to do with Jeff Bezos' company, but was the first lesbian/feminist bookstore in the US, named after the Amazons, a mythological tribe of fierce and independent women. After decades in business, the organization sold its name to Amazon.com to avoid lengthy and costly court battles over naming rights.

Digital co-operatives generally don't join the NCBA and they don't pay dues, so they lead an ephemeral existence outside the world of brick-and-mortar co-ops – but that doesn't mean they can't play a vital role. At first glance the idea of self-help, self-responsibility and self-administration, as well as trust and reliability, fundamental to all co-operatives seems to fit the Web like a glove. One possible alternative might be digital labor unions which we will explore now.

Digital co-determination

If history has taught us anything, it is that if enough people get together and agree to change something, they will succeed. From the French to the Russian revolutions and, indeed, the United States own version fought to free the colony from its English overlords, to the Workers' Movements during the 19th century, the student revolts of the mid-20th century, and the fall of the Berlin Wall in June 1990: every time pressure builds up past a certain point, the valves fly off, the power of the masses is unleashed, and transformation happens – for better or for worse.

Sometimes steam is let off in a controlled and orderly fashion but that isn't always the case. In fact, it was because workers worried about the horrendous events in the aftermath of the French Revolution that Social Democratic parties were formed in 19th century Europe. Trades unions are also part of this development. At the time when American farmers were heading for points west in droves, European workers were gathering in groups and protesting a wide range of perceived injustices. The strike in 1829 of several thousand journeymen in Germany, also known as the Weberaufstand (the Rising of the Weavers), signaled the start of a period of intense worker unionization, and from about 1848 –still smack in the middle of the Wild West in the US – national trades unions were formed along the lines of the traditional guild fraternities. Unions gave workers their first opportunity to negotiate with the bosses from a position of equality.

In the digital age, trades unions are struggling but they still have important roles to play and to remain relevant, union organizers will have to face up to the new reality. For one thing, they and management, long-used to collective bargaining (usually behind closed doors and presenting agreements the rank and file of workers are expected to wave through), will need to accept new partners at the bargaining table. As we move towards a gig economy, freelances will want a say and new ways of working towards a social pact will have to be adopted, possibly by some system of crowdsourcing and online participation.

At a national conference of trades unionists hosted by the German Trade Union Confederation (DGB), one delegate rose and asked whether Facebook would be the perfect alternative to old-fashion trades unions. After all, he said, if enough angry people flood the

Facebook page of an unfair employer, it would generate at least as much outrage and attention as a few dozen people marching around waving placards and posters in front of the company's headquarters.

But why stop there?

Organizing digital labor

In a way, we all work for GAFA. We create content for Facebook to sell, we let Google spy on our online habits and create personal profiles of us to peddle to the highest bidder who then bombards us with extremely well-targeted ads. We tell Amazon exactly what we want so they can sell us more of it or even suggest stuff we might not have thought of buying. And the longer we stare into the screens of our iPhones, the more money Apple makes – after all, attention is the most precious commodity there is in the Digital Age.

So, if we're working for them anyway, why don't we get paid? Surely only slaves work for free and, as toilers in the fields of GAFA, we have a right to be compensated. If the bosses don't like the idea, then we need to organize, just as the workers in the Gilded Age when labor unions began forming to counter the social and economic impact of the Industrial Revolution and the rise of the mega-trusts. The Knights of Labor emerged in the US in the late 1880s, and the American Federation of Labor was founded in 1886. Both helped co-ordinate and support local strikes and eventually became a political force to be reckoned with during the New Deal of the 1930s and later on.

So why don't we have digital unions forcing GAFA & Co to sign collective bargaining agreements with us?

There are many reasons, of course, including differences in nationality and language, the lack of common legal and cultural frameworks, and reluctance on the part of the politicians to go after the internet giants, mainly because they don't understand the dangers we face from them. But, most of all, GAFA has managed to brainwash us into blindly accepting their handouts in the form of a few free apps and some neat services while hiding their true cost from us in every way they can.

No one needs to be a prophet or a rocket scientist to predict that many of us will lose their jobs to robots and artificial intelligence (AI). Experts disagree about how many there will wind up on the digital dole, and naturally, there will be new jobs created through technology, but one thing is certain: it will be the poorly educated and badly paid who will be the first to go. Who needs supermarket clerks if all they do is drag stuff over a barcode scanner if a robot can do it faster and more efficiently? Or if we can simply order and pay for our groceries online and just stop by our local AmazonGo store to pick them up on our way home?

One study by scientists from the University of Oxford in the UK warned that 47 percent of total US employment is at risk of being replaced by machines. The list of endangered professions include data entry clerks, truck and delivery van drivers, restaurant chefs, lawyers and financial analysts (not that we'll miss them), telemarketers and customer service assistants, medics, construction workers, musicians and artists, and bartenders. On the other hand, skilled workers and specialists will be in greater demand than ever before.

The sad truth is that the unqualified are screwed! In the digital economy there is less and less room for mediocrity. Companies are screaming out for talent, talent, talent, but the wells are mostly dry. In Europe and Japan, this is largely due to demographics and the fact that the Baby Boomer generation was too busy to have kids. As a result, the so-called age pyramid in developed countries like Germany (see illustration) look more like a mushroom: thick head, slender body. So far, Americans have proven fecund enough to keep the pyramid relatively stable and the offspring coming, but with unemployment touching record lows, US companies too are desperate for qualified workers.

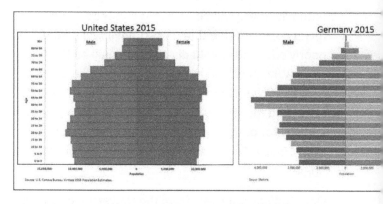

The good news for those who have work is that jobs will be more fun. Automation eliminates the dangerous, boring, humdrum, and repetitive tasks, such as SAM, a bricklaying robot from Construction Robotics, which is already hard at work in New York State and can lay courses of bricks six times faster than any human. What remains are the challenging tasks as well as jobs only humans are fit for because they require ingenuity, creativity or empathy.

A September 2018 study entitled *Cognitive Diversity: AI and the Future of Work*, published by Ken Goldberg, a professor at the University of California,

Berkeley, and Vinod Kumar, CEO of Tata
Communications, surveyed 120 senior executives.
About 77 percent of them believed that AI would
increase the number of roles, rather than replace
existing positions. Around 57 percent of respondents
choose both options, that AI can produce more roles
but will take away others. This will mean companies
need to proactively train their workforces today in
order to fill their talent requirement tomorrow.

This should not really come as a big surprise, if past
experience is anything to go by. Technological
advances like barcode scanners and ATM machines
took away time-consuming tasks and freed-up
employees to work more efficiently and in a timely
manner. Other jobs that could benefit from AI include
truck driving. After all, airline pilots have been relying
for decades on their autopilots to fly aircraft over
long distances, but inevitably take control themselves
during takeoff and landing or in stress situations. Why
shouldn't truckers sit back and relax on long hauls
and grab the wheel only when called on to navigate
narrow urban streets and alleys?

AI is already entering office life where help with
complex and tedious tasks like managing supply
chains, allocating desk space, and keeping records of
meetings. An article in *The Economist* argues that "all
this can free up time for people to work on more
important strategic decisions". It also states that AI
could make collaboration within companies easier,
for instance by getting rid of language barriers.
Multinational companies often have employees
lacking a common language; AI could handle
translation in real time to make dialogue easier.

In the end, AI may also be a way of avoiding
"groupthink"; a tendency for team members within

large companies to develop similar cognitive patters which eventually become part of the corporate DNA. Smart algorithms could conceivably act as irritants, causing the human colleagues to think anew before making a potentially disastrous decision just because "that's the way we've always done things here".

What about those people who fall through the cracks; those who are simply unemployable in a digital economy, because the lack the required "tools" though birth defects, low IQs or various mental disorders that make them at best suited to humdrum jobs but not to the brave new working world? The best course would be, of course, an unconditional basic income (UBI) for all, effectively separating work and wages from one another. In a society that makes sure its citizens are guaranteed a dignified existence with no strings attached, people without the chance to engage in rewarding work could turn to other forms of ungainful employment, for instance community work, taking care of elderly family members, or art. Real old-fashioned jobs would only be for those lucky enough to possess the necessary skills and competencies and would be regarded as a lucky break.

Attempts at introducing UBI, sometimes also referred to as a demogrant, distributed to every citizen automatically without the need to notify the authorities about any change in an individual's financial situation, have met with varying degrees of success in the past. Considered part of a post-capitalist economic system, it has come under heavy criticism from the right-wing and often with only half-hearted support from liberals. In fact, the idea goes as far back as 16th century England, when Sir Thomas More, a counselor to Henry VIII, argued in his *Utopia* that every person should receive an assured income.

In the early 1920s, philosopher Bertrand Russell tried to establish a social movement for basic income in the United Kingdom.

Since the turn of this millennium, basic income has again become an active topic in many countries. Experiments in India in 2016 and Canada in 2018, for example, have received international media attention. Finland adopted a limited program in 2017 but refused to extend it to all citizens in 2018 after a change of government, choosing to explore alternative welfare schemes instead. Several countries have used polls to investigate public support for basic income. In 2016, 76.9 percent of Swiss voters in a national referendum rejected a basic income proposal. In February 2018, Gallup pollsters found Americans split on universal income for workers displaced by AI, with 48percent in favor and 52 percent opposed.

So, if governments can't make up their minds, why not force the big tech companies to ante up? After all, they're the ones making obscenely large profits by putting people out of work with their smart robots, self-learning algorithms and general automation.

Attempts to introduce machine taxes aren't new, either. During World War II, the Nazis outlawed automated cigar rolling machines to protect the incomes of farmers' wives who moonlighted in cigar factories in southwestern Germany. None less that Bill Gates, one of the world's richest individuals, proposed a robot tax in 2017 intended to "ease the inequality and offset the social costs implied by automation's displacement effects", as he said in an interview with Yanis Varoufakis, the economist who served as the Greek Minister of Finance in 2015. Gates' proposal, one of many variants on the UBI theme, allows us to glimpse fascinating aspects of capitalism and human nature that rich societies have neglected for too long, Varoufakis declares. The head of the German postal service Frank Appel is on record as demanding a tax on robots exclusively, doing away with income taxes for humans. "If a human being has to sort letters by hand, then something is wrong," he claimed in an interview with *Die Welt*. The European Parliament's Committee on Legal Affairs went further when it recently called for a value added tax on robots and AI, as well as requiring them to pay social security.

Yet another idea is for a fixed portion of all new stock market issues (IPOs) to go into a public trust that, in turn, would generates an income stream from which a UBI could be paid. That way, society effectively would become a shareholder in every corporation, the dividends to be distributed evenly to all citizens.

Digital workers council

Okay, so there is no lack of ideas but how do we ensure Big Tech's co-operation? How about employee participation? This generally means that employees share an activity with a team of managers, collectively taking responsibility for the outcome (such as the completion of some goal or sticking to a timetable.) The team provides the forum where employees can suggest ideas to make the project run more efficiently and make decisions about their portion of the team's project. These schemes, popular with human resources departments everywhere, are intended to actively encourage the work force to assist in running and improving the business and in having a say in important management decisions, and they normally involve extra compensation: the employee share. This can consist of a cash payment at the end of the year or an option to purchase company stock at a dividend.

Since we all now work for GAFA in one way or the other, as discussed above, why shouldn't we get a bonus once or twice a year? After all, we are heavily invested in terms of time and attention in what these companies are doing, so why shouldn't we demand our fair share?

This won't happen by itself, we will need to apply pressure. Probably the best solution would be a kind of digital workers council, a body representing the interests of customers and users all over the world. In some countries, workplace representation is firmly ensconced with employees given the right to effectively veto some issues.

Yes, we will need to work out lots of details, such as how companies can be forced to accept this kind of public participation, who gets to sit on the council, and how they are elected (by universal suffrage of all netizens – in which case, will people in authoritarian states be allowed to vote their conscience or will they be forced to follow the party line and other similar issues). The best bet will probably be to turn it over to an international body such as the United Nations, or maybe something like the Internet Corporation for Assigned Names and Numbers (ICANN) or the Internet Engineering Task Force (IETF), a non-profit organization of loosely affiliated international participants that lets anyone contribute to its technical expertise. Another way would be to upgrade the Internet Governance Forum (IGF), established in 2005 by the World Summit on the Information Society (WSIS), which has subsequently broadened its brief beyond narrow technical concerns to include a wider range of internet-related policy issues. All it lacks is teeth but, if the UN put its weight behind it, the bite of WSIS could maybe one day become stronger than its bark.

A new moral compass for the Digital Age

Such a council would also need to reach agreement with GAFA and others about the rules both sides are to follow. For such a playbook to be written, we first need to come up with a broader sense of what is right and not; an updated moral compass; in short: an ethical system that doesn't conflict with the goals we set ourselves as a society in order to create the kind of future we all want to live in.

"Technology has no ethics – but human society depend upon ethics," says Gerd Leonhard. As technology progresses exponentially, our rules and regulations which were arrived at long ago in a linear society no longer fit and need to be updated.

Instead of asking how we can draw the most profit out of technological advances, we should be asking why we need them in the first place and what things like AI and self-learning algorithms, self-driving cars and self-automating systems will mean for humanity in the long run. And we need to start soon, before our machines become smarter than us and begin to take over decision-making in areas far beyond our human understanding – and control!

Exponential technologies tend to pass through three stages, Leonhard maintains: first magic, then manic, and finally toxic. Since all of this is happening at digital speed, finding the right balance and deciding where to call a stop gets more difficult every day. He therefore calls for a Global Digital Ethics Council which he would like to see established under the aegis of the UN and consisting of people from all walks of life; normal citizens, academics, governments, business and technology companies, as well as "free-thinkers", as he calls them: writers, artists, and intellectuals from various fields and schools of thought. Their job would be to serve as an early warning system endowed with the authority to monitor and, when necessary, inform the public about potentially harmful, illegal or immoral developments in technology.

But first, of course, we need to agree what constitutes morality in the Digital Age. Which school of ethics should we be following? In his book *Machines of Loving Grace*, John Markoff, an American journalist, writes: "Today, decisions about implementing technology are made largely on the basis of profitability and efficiency." It would be truly surprising, he believes, if a Silicon Valley company rejected a profitable technology for ethical reasons – but that is exactly what needs to happen if we don't want the boat we are all sitting in to go on the rocks.

Charlotte de Broglie, CEO and founder of For The Future, a French consulting company based in Paris, helps her clients develop strategies for digital transformation. She bemoans the fact that most companies focus shortsightedly on utility over social, economic and cultural considerations that reflect real human needs. Something needs to change, she believes, and we should start in our schools, during vocational training and at our colleges and universities. The digital thought leaders, developers of new digital solutions and products, mathematicians, engineers and computerologists of tomorrow should be given a firm interdisciplinary grounding in technology assessment, says de Broglie.

"Unless digital actors, and, indeed, all citizens, are given the means to ponder, develop and foster an autonomous vision that reflects their values, we will inevitably drift towards digital autocracy," she told delegates to the OECD (Organisation for Economic Co-operation and Development) Forum in 2016. "If all hope of an independent vision of digital technology is abandoned, its applications will ultimately be dictated by all-powerful multinationals, thereby strengthening their grip and adding to global imbalances, especially in the area of internet governance," she concluded.

Digital technologies should be part of a bigger picture that needs to be patiently and carefully developed by theorists, scientists, engineers, digital creators and civil society in order to co-construct an empowering ethical dialogue and discourse. In the area of human-computer interaction, there can, and should be, a systematic ethical encounter, without slowing the momentum of innovation.

Can machines be moral?

Digital ethics can be put to entirely practical uses, of course. One area where demand for "machine ethics" is growing involves autonomous vehicles, in other words self-driving cars, trucks, and busses. When I asked a friend of mine, Janina Loh, a charming young professor of philosophy at the University of Vienna about this, she laughed: "Okay, but which school of ethics do you mean – there are so many of them!" In her new book *Trans- and Posthumanism*, she cites the now-famous Trolley Problem, a thought experiment in ethics first proposed by the British philosopher Phillipa Foot, in which she tried to demonstrate the difficulty of asking machines to reach moral decisions. It goes like this:

You see a runaway trolley moving toward five tied-up (or otherwise incapacitated) people lying on the tracks. You are standing next to a lever that controls a switch. If you pull the lever, the trolley will be redirected onto a side track and the five people on the main track will be saved. However, there is a single person lying on the side track. You have two options:

1. *Do nothing and allow the trolley to kill the five people on the main track.*
2. *Pull the lever, diverting the trolley onto the side track where it will kill one person.*

Which is the most ethical option?

Common sense says pull the damn lever, and be quick about it! And in fact, philosophy, or at least the philosophical school known as Utilitarianism which is very popular in the US, would demand that you do so. According to Jeremy Bentham (1748-1832), the founder of the Utilitarianist school, a decision is morally defensible if it leads to the "greatest good for the greatest number".

Another approach would be by purpose-oriented ethics, or 'ethics of action' dictated by the deontological ethics of Immanuel Kant, the famous 18th century German enlightenment philosopher. In his major work, *The Critique of Pure Reason* (1781), Kant argues that taking a human life, regardless of the circumstances, is immoral.

What began as a funny thought experiment was suddenly thrust to the fore in March 2018 when the long-expected happened: a self-driving Uber car ran over and killed a pedestrian crossing a street in in

Tempe, Arizona - the first fatal accident of its kind. Immediately, calls came for a built-in system of ethical decision making, but of course, no one mentioned which kind of ethics they meant.

Almost as tricky to answer is the question of liability. Who should pay in a case like this? The car's programmer? Uber? The person sitting in the car but not actually in control of it at the time? Or should it be attributed to *force majeure*; an unforeseeable circumstance?

Take your pick – and, in fact, we may soon be forced to. Machine ethics is less a technological and more a societal problem. Lawyers may squabble over who is to blame and whether it's time to bring our traffic laws up to date but, at the end of the day, it will be us, the citizens of the Digital Age, who decide what we think is right and should be enshrined in law.

Janina Loh calls for mandatory ethics classes in schools and universities. "We can't put this off for coming generations to decide," she says. "We need to educate people at various levels here and now in order to create ethical awareness!" Similarly, she feels tech companies, especially those engaged in AI development, should be required to offer their employees ethics training to make up for the lack of such instruction during their educational upbringing. Finally, she concludes that all big companies should be obliged to establish ethics commissions, such as those already mandated by law in some US States or by various county and city ordinances, to investigate dishonest or unethical practices by public employees and elected officials.

So, besides digital rights and opportunities, we find that we also have digital obligations; the most

important being to help shape our common future
and create rules which we must follow if society is to
survive.

Chapter 6: 10 lessons from the Wild West

"We must get used
to the idea that the standardized internet is the past
but not the future."

Eli Noam

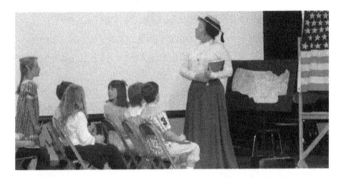

I owe my readers a personal word of explanation at this point. For one thing, all my forefathers were protestant ministers of one denomination or another, ever since my ancestor James Cole moved to Plymouth, Massachusetts, in 1633, just 13 years after the Mayflower landed. While any religious hankering I may have felt as a youngster has long since faded, I have never managed to shake off what the philosopher Max Weber (1864-1920) described as the protestant work ethic, which states that we are only what we make of ourselves and that our actions can lead to change for the better.

For another, I carry the heady "spirit of '68" inside me. In the summer of 1968 protest movements among students broke out everywhere in the West, from the Sorbonne in Paris to Columbia and Barnard

Universities in America. The trouble spread to Heidelberg in Germany, where I went to school and later attended classes for US soldiers and dependents at the European branch of the University of Maryland (Dad was a US Air Force chaplain who met my mother during the final weeks of World War II and took her home as a kind of war booty!).

In the street fighting in Heidelberg, I was sprayed by water cannon and beaten up by riot policemen. I adored politicians like the Social Democrats Willi Brandt and Helmut Schmidt, and I cried when they gunned down Rudi Dutschke in front of a drugstore in Berlin.

The reason I set all this down is to explain why, in my humble opinion, it is time to strike back!

In '68 we were all proud to belong to the so-called extra-parliamentary opposition, or APO as it is known in Germany, but even then the progressive forces were drifting slowly apart. There were those, among whom I count myself, who believed in gradual, democratically-legitimized change, in what we called "the long march through the institutions".

Then there were others for whom change wasn't happening fast enough and who slowly drifted into active resistance and terrorism. One of these was Ulrike Meinhof, who I knew to be a relatively moderate bluestocking in Frankfurt, but who later got to know Andreas Baader. Baader had been convicted of arson in Berlin and, together with his sidekick Jan Raspe and the radical socialist Gudrun Ensslin, went on to found the Red Army Faction, also known as the Baader-Meinhof Gang, which committed numerous bank robberies and bombings. The gang was captured in 1972 and sent to jail in Stuttgart, the city where I also happened to live at the time, and all four committed suicide in their cells in 1975.

Anyone who went through these troubled times, as I did, with open eyes, knows how deeply these events affected all of society. It also served as a lesson on the need, from time to time, for civil disobedience to act as an engine of change and showed how quickly large swaths of people in a normally staid and steady country like Germany can be radicalized almost overnight. I worry that history may repeat itself.

If proof were needed that people today will take to the streets if they feel their digital rights are in jeopardy, we only need to look back to the cold winter of 2011, when demonstrators gathered in many major European cities to protest against the Anti-Counterfeiting Trade Agreement (ACTA). The pact was thrashed out behind closed doors by representatives of the United States, the European Union and Japan and was intended to put a stop to digital piracy and the illegal copying of music and videos. Online activists saw this as an attempt to take away their right to share legally obtained content with friends and acquaintances (which it was). They objected specifically to allowing media companies to take the law into their own hands by locking copycats out of their systems, or even taking away their internet access completely. Rallies were organized and protest marches held, with chants of "ACTA ad acta" (which roughly translates as "close the file on ACTA") and "stop the media mafia" echoing through the freezing streets of Germany, including Munich where I lived.

Between February and June of 2012, more than 200,000 protesters in 200 cities vented their anger at ACTA. The German government was the first to cave-in, declaring themselves unwilling to sign the final agreement. Other nations followed and, in July 4, 2012 – Independence Day in the US, no less – the European Parliament voted against ACTA by 478 to 39 votes, with 165 abstentions.

Now, as everyone knows, the European Union isn't really a democratic institution, and parliament doesn't have the last word. Delegates tend to keep voting until the desired result is achieved, and so it was this time. ACTA was well and truly buggered, as they say in Britain, but the devious publishers and media sneaks didn't give up that easily. They persuaded their friends in the Byzantine corridors of Brussels to introduce almost the same Bill once again, only this time they called it "copyright reform" which of course is not about the right to copy but about the publishers right to stop people from copying stuff they have purchased legally. And, just to make sure nobody got to share their digital content with friends or acquaintances (as they would physically lend a book or a record), the powers-that-be introduced the requirement for online platforms to implement so-called upload filters – which is exactly what the Chinese government has been doing for decades following the introduction of the Great Firewall of China.

The net effect was that the creation of a kind of global symmetry and digital censorship has now become a worldwide norm – or it will be by the time this book is published. I just hope you, gentle reader, will have gotten your copy of this before they let the robots loose to decide who gets to download it and who doesn't.

At Re:publica 2018, a media conference in Berlin, John Weitzmann of Wikimedia Germany called the copyright reform a thinly-disguised attempt to further centralize the internet. The reform act, he believes, will make the big platforms, like GAFA, even bigger and thus easier for state agencies like America's National Security Agency (NSA) to monitor and control. You thought Big Brother was already watching you? You ain't seen nothing yet!

The Copyright Reform Act is a huge setback for digital human-rights activists and others who hoped they had made their point by defeating ACTA and were home safe. Crushing ACTA has only proven to be a battle won, not a war, but it does have its repercussions to this day. For instance, at the height of the ACTA protests, the Internet Defense League (IDL) was born. According to Tiffiniy Cheng, co-founder of Fight for the Future, the IDL's parent organization, the aim of the site is to sign up thousands of other websites, from giant organizations to individual bloggers, who can be mobilized quickly, if needed, for future anti-piracy legislation protests. The organization will use a "cat signal", a take on the fictional Bat signal used to summon Batman, if there is need to act. "There's this academic theory ... that talks about: if you ban the ability of people to share cat photos, they'll start protesting en masse," Cheng says to explain why IDL chose the symbol of a cat.

Maybe it's time to start posting cat photos again.

Solidarity, Society and Sovereignty

Historians generally agree that the reason for the decline and downfall of the Native American population was due to the superior weapons the European invaders brought with them – as though the redskins, as they were called, were some primitive race incapable of matching the achievements of Western civilization. They conveniently forget that the Mayan civilization of Central America, for example, created a sophisticated body of mathematical and astronomical knowledge that was at least as developed as anything the West had to offer, and that they had, in fact, invented the concept of 0 (zero) around 300BCE, long before the scholars in India who are usually credited with it today. Of course, without 0 we wouldn't have a binary system today: no computers, no internet, no World Wide Web – so there, palefaces!

What's more, Native American tribes had already developed a complex culture based on collaboration and social co-operation. The Iroquois and Huron tribes cultivated the land in common, but with each tribe acting autonomously. Important decisions, like when to start the planting season, were reached by mutual consent. To hunt wild buffalo, Cheyenne and Dakota hunters would work together to ride the big herds over the nearest cliff where the beasts fell to their deaths by the thousands. These so-called Buffalo Jumps called for a great degree of autonomy and self-organization by the tribes.

Collaboration? Self-organization? Autonomy? Aren't those words we hear a lot today in the Digital Age?

Whose data are they, anyway?

We live in a world of data today but, unfortunately, nobody really knows who rightly owns the information. This issue isn't as trivial as it may sound. The European Convention on Human Rights says in Article 8: "Everyone has the right to respect for his private and family life, his home and his correspondence." Legal scholars argue that this means the right of the individual to decide what personal information should be communicated to others and under what circumstances, marking a sharp contradiction to the United States where, according to legal tradition, the "right to privacy" is simply the "right to be left alone". The closest the US Constitution comes to privacy protection is the Fourth Amendment which only protects persons and their belongings from warrantless search. So, if it's still unclear to whom my data belongs, the Fourth Amendment isn't any help at all.

People are very sensitive about these issues, especially in Germany, a country with a difficult history of state-sponsored surveillance, first by the Nazis and then, in East Germany, by the Communists,. In 1981, before re-unification, when the government in West Germany decided to conduct a census, civil rights activists went to court – and won! The poll was postponed and, on December 15, 1983, the Constitutional High Court sent down its historic *Volkszählungsurteil* (Census Decision), and it wasn't until 1987 that the Big Count could finally take place, albeit with a completely redesigned questionnaire that separated personal from purely statistical data with the assurance the results would be anonymous.

All this was long before surveillance cameras, face-recognition systems and geolocation via smartphone, and we need to remember at this point that computers were still pretty much in their infancy in those days. IBM had launched its very first Personal Computer in 1981, and large computers, such as those operated by state agencies, still relied largely on punched cards and ticker tape. Even so, the High Court judges worried about what computers might one day be capable of doing. They argued that, if citizens could neither know nor influence what information about them was stored and kept available, they would modify their behavior out of fear. This would weigh on their individual freedom to act and would harm society as a whole because the free and democratic community depends on the self-determined collaboration of all its citizens.

In 1983, Roland Appel published a book entitled *Careful, Census!* (*Vorsicht Volkszählung!*) which inflamed public opinion in the days leading up to the historic decision. Looking back after a quarter of a century, he told me: "It was a big step forward but back then all the state needed to do was confiscate a few punch cards, magnetic tapes or disk drives to make sure everybody was following the law. Today, things are totally different. Democratic government's monopoly of power is being challenged by search engines and internet providers. Just like back in days of the Wild West, we citizens really have no other choice but to take matters into our own hands. Our best protection is no longer the Colt, but a secure browser, software and an operating system that is safe from intrusion by strangers, be they criminals or agencies of foreign countries – or our own!"

Not all data are created equal

The Open Data Institute defines three separate forms of data: closed, shared, and open. In most debates about data privacy, these distinctions are ignored. In fact, it should be clear to everyone that not all data are created equal. If we want to have an informed conversation about data, their use and misuse, we need to accept that, in most cases, multiple parties are involved in their creation, processing, distribution and storage.

Nowadays, the big data debate is full of contradictions. There are those who say data are the "crude oil of the 21st century", a valuable asset, which means that data will play an important role in creating wealth and economic growth. Others are afraid of data, which they associate with data theft, attacks on data, and thought police. For these people, data are something we hand over to the state or the social web platforms which then turn around and use them to spy on us. Either that, or the data fall into the hands of hoodlums who try to steal them from us and use them for their nefarious purposes. Either way, you must protect your data by building walls (firewalls) around them.

A big proponent of this walled-garden approach to the internet is my old friend Jaron Lanier, who turned from Paul back to Saul by renouncing his former allegiance to tech (he was one of the early, but largely unsuccessful, players in the virtual reality industry back in the 1990s). He recently wrote a book entitled *Ten Arguments for Deleting Your Social Media Accounts Right Now.* That's pure baloney! No one can turn back the clock and, instead of lamenting, we should be seeking ways to take back our sovereignty over the data we produce.

Sovereignty has a nice ring to it, containing as it does the word 'sovereign', which implies an almost regal dominance as well as autonomy and independence, but also of calmness and equanimity. We definitely must learn to deal with our data in a sovereign way.

Each of us produces masses of data every day. Our smartphones are constantly creating movement profiles without us knowing it. The Fitbit you wear on your wrist is constantly monitoring and recording your vital statistics. Let these data fall into the wrong hands – say, your health insurance company – and you might find yourself uninsured because of an unknown previously-existing condition. You can thank

Donald Trump and his buddies in Congress for that, by the way.

When you take your car, which nowadays might best be described as a 'smartphone on wheels', to a garage, the maintenance guy usually hooks it up to a computer that extracts tons of data that the car has gathered from countless built-in sensors. This data is then transmitted to the car's manufacturer, who uses them to develop new and better cars, but also to create services he can sell you – just like Apple does with the iPhone (whose purchase price, as outrageously high as it is, is just a tiny part of the revenue stream it generates for Apple from the apps and services sold over months and years). Nobody asks you if this is okay; they simply assume they have the right to take all your data they can eat because its free!

The only reason they can get away with this hoggish behavior is because we have not created binding moral norms governing the use of personal data. The best example in recent times was the Cambridge Analytica scandal where the marketing company, in partnership with Facebook, was found to have siphoned off the data of at least 87 million users and sent the information, in duly processed form, to Donald Trump's election team who then used it to massively influence voter choices during the elections of 2016. The reaction from politicians was typical: first, quickly cover your ass; then, ignore the whole thing.

To win back sovereignty over our data, we will need to take action. It probably isn't too late to devise a new social contract for the Digital Age; a set of mutually agreed rules and regulations that protect and empower us as individuals. One could be that we will respect digital privacy the same way we do physical integrity: After all, we don't intrude ourselves into someone else's personal space by getting too close – and if we do so, #metoo is making such behavior increasingly unacceptable, both morally and legally. 'Bout time, too!

Kevin Keith of *GovHack*, a kind of open data hackathon in Australia, calls for a social contract that will allow us to donate our data to something that is bigger than any of us. His goal is to establish an ongoing dialogue between governments, business and civil society that will create enhanced data awareness in each of them long after the dust of the Cambridge Analytica affair has settled.

There are a few hopeful signs that this may be happening at the moment. Acxiom, the world's biggest data broker, has been collecting information about every single one of us since 1969 which it sells to advertisers wishing to set up personalized ad campaigns. They have so-called 'personal profiles' of just about everybody, including very personal details, for instance, about our financial and marital status, purchasing preferences and where we live – including information about who else lives in our neighborhood and whether they pay their bills on time of not; assuming, of course, that if you live on the wrong side of the tracks, you, too, may constitute a credit risk. This is called scoring, and it can be astonishingly accurate.

Above all, everything Acxiom knows about you comes from perfectly legal sources like land registries, credit agencies, and increasingly from websites. Every time we open a web browser and wander with our computer mouse across a page, we are leaving tracks that can be gathered by companies that specialize in such things. One of the tricks of the trade is installing so-called tracking pixels, tiny, invisible bugging devices, on web pages that gather information about us and send it to information harvesters like Acxiom.

There are lots of companies in the same business as Acxiom, and they are all constantly watching us when we go online, whether we actually do anything there or not. Google and Facebook do the same, and if you would like to know what Facebook, for instance, knows about you, all you need to do is log into your Facebook account and type in the following URL: *www.facebook.com/ads/preferences*. You will immediately be transferred to a page entitled "Your ad preferences", and there you will find a list of keywords Facebook has culled from your past visits to its site. Fortunately, it turns out that Facebook is a rank amateur compared to Acxiom when it comes to creating meaningful personal profiles.

According to Facebook, I am interested in, among other things, "traditional Chinese medicine". That was news to me but, presumably, at some point in the past I stumbled across something on Facebook dealing with things like Shiatsu, Qigong, herbal medicine, or Ayurveda. At least that's what it says in my list. For one thing, Ayurveda is from India, not China, but maybe Facebook is staffed by average American high school students who are famously weak in geography, a subject no longer taught in some States (in 2014, three-quarters of eight-graders tested below proficiency in geography, according to the National Assessment of Educational Progress – also known as the Nation's Report Card).

Anyway, Asian medication is not very high on my personal priority list but Facebook begs to differ. Heaven help the advertisers who pay good money for my personal profile and adjust their messages to fit – they will be instantly deleted!

Acxiom does a much better job. I know this because they let me peek into their database. No, I am not a hacker; they allowed me to. In September 2013, CEO Scott Howe announced an initiative called *aboutthedata.com* which gives everyone the opportunity to access the information Acxiom has gathered about them and see if everything is correct. If not, we even get to correct the entry any way we want.

Actually, that poses a problem because, people being what they are, sometimes lie. Ladies lie about their age and men exaggerate. Both affectations are bad for the reliability of the results. Acxiom has hit upon what I think is an ingenious solution: We get to say what we believe is the truth, but the previous information remains visible. The advertisers that purchase our profiles get to decide who they think is right. If they choose wrongly, their ads will bounce off into cyberspace.

Wouldn't it be nice if, for instance, the NSA gave us the same option? Just don't hold your breath...

At the online press conference Acxiom gave to publicize their new arrangement, I asked Howe why he decided to give away his crown jewels, so to speak, namely all the well-guarded information that the company presumably spent a fortune gathering. He was very upfront about it. "We are beginning to feel the heat from regulators all over the world, so we know that at some point we will be forced to open up. So we decided it's better to be part of the solution than part of the problem."

Google and the others would be well advised to take a page out of Acxiom's book.

Could this usher in a new era in dealing with our data? It really looks like it. In the summer of 2018, Microsoft, Facebook, Google, and Twitter announced their Data Transfer Project which is intended to make shifting personal data back and forth between online platforms easier – or, in fact, possible for the first time ever. Switching platforms, especially cloud platforms, has been extremely difficult in the past. Riches or a crown may not be forever but, once you signed up with GAFA and such, you have a hard time getting out with your data intact.

All that is supposed to change now with the Data Transfer Project. Packing your pictures up on Instagram and copying them over to Flickr should soon be as easy as moving them to a new folder on your disk drive. Basically, this is what politicians have been demanding for quite some time, especially in Europe (see Chapter 3), namely: open-interfaced data portability. Users should be allowed to move as often as they want, these people say – and even be allowed to make everything on Facebook, for example, go away. At the moment, this right is restricted to the four major players mentioned above, but others are sure to join them over time. And, who knows, maybe one day this will become a new world standard.

In an interview with the *Süddeutsche Zeitung* newspaper, data security expert Paul Olivier Dehaye says this is a good first step but he thinks it falls short of what is really needed. The really important stuff, he believes, isn't kept with the rest of our personal data but has long-since become part of the GAFA's mighty algorithms where they are impossible to extract or even access.

Similar criticism has been leveled against Acxiom's attempt at opening their databases. On *aboutthedata.com*, all we get to see is our basic profile and not the conclusions Acxiom draws from them. They, however, are what advertisers are so keen to get their grubby little hands on. For instance, Acxiom can tell if you are a "potential inheritor", if you live in a household with a "diabetic focus" or "senior needs", or whether you are an "adult with senior parent". Jeff Chester, executive director of the Center for Digital Democracy believes this is "nothing but a first small step in the right direction".

10 things the Wild West teaches us

In the course of writing this book I have attempted to show the many parallels between the short, and violent age of the Wild West and the no less-rough and stormy early days of the World Wide Web, the early days of which are with us still because, in historic terms, the web has only been around for the blink of an eye, even if you measure it in Internet Years (dog years?). We all need to constantly remind ourselves that this is only the beginning of a long and turbulent journey, and it is up to all of us to shape the course and determine, if there is one, the final destination.

To get there will require plenty of effort: we need to correct the mistakes we made and tame the beasts that we have nurtured at our bosoms. Here, of course, I'm talking about GAFA and their ilk; monster companies that have managed to amass more power over our lives than any before in the history of the world. They must be pruned back and, probably, broken up for the good of mankind because they are leading us into an Eloi-like existence that will be hard to distinguish from slavery, and the worst thing is that we are in the process of self-abdication. Neither machines nor GAFA want to take power over us; we are in danger of simply handling over that power without a struggle.

At the end, I want to offer up a list of 10 lessons I believe we all should learn from how the West was won in order to shape a better future for us, the citizens of the Digital Age. And I firmly believe that we, too, will win in the end.

1. In the stormy days of '68, the slogan we marched under was: "Destroy what destroys you!". In light of the excessive power of GAFA and the others, it will be important for the future of humanity to rein them in – probably to break them up or even destroy them if they put up too much resistance. In the cases of Google/Alphabet and Facebook, the historic precedents are crystal clear: Standard Oil and AT&T needed to be dismantled, like pruning back an apple tree grown into disarray.

   This will result in dozens of independent companies, each dealing with a different aspect of technology. Each, presumably, capable of holding its own in a competitive market without needing to hold on to the apron strings of a gigantic corporate parent, wildly exchanging tons of personal data from entirely different businesses that just happen to belong under its roof.

2. The World Wide Web and its major players need adult supervision! There are enough suggestions making the rounds, from a Digital Rights Board described above to a kind of

quality label preferably issued by a private-public partnership. One example of such a body is the German TÜV which, for the past 100 years, has been tasked with certifying the roadworthiness of cars and trucks.

Viktor Mayer-Schönberger, an Austria-born legalist and head of the Oxford Internet Institute, has called for mandatory data exchange which would be graded by the size of the company, kicking in at somewhere around 10 percent market share. Above that, tech companies should be forced to share the data they have harvested from consumers with other, especially smaller, companies to create a level playing field and avoid stifling innovation which would only lead to big companies getting even bigger.

3. Society needs rule of law to function properly. It was no different in the days of the Wild West than it is today – and laws are the responsibility of governments. However, we also need social rules and principles that help us maintain civility and fairness among ourselves without the need for any higher authority to interfere. In the early days of the internet, we, as users, made our own rules and called it 'netiquette'. Today, the call for a kind of digital commonsense is gaining in volume and we are all summoned to put it into practice.

We will need to establish a new set of moral and ethical guidelines that can help us shape the digital future so the result will be the kind of world we all want to live in. We need to communicate these digital ethics aggressively within our communities: in schools and universities, in training facilities and, above all, within our companies. I agree with Janina Loh that every large company should have an ethics officer, similar to the privacy officer required by law in many countries in Europe.

4. Laws are only as good as the politicians who make them. That was no different back in the Wild West than it is today. Helmut Kohl, the German chancellor who oversaw reunification in the 1980s, was asked in later years what he thought about the data highway, to which he replied: "Road building is a State matter!" Nearly two decades later, his successor Angela Merkel gave a speech at the opening of CeBIT 2013 in which she stated: "The internet is virgin territory for us."

Yes, a civilized nation needs laws, but it also needs politicians who know what the hell they are about. The internet needs regulation, for sure, but that will require skill and tact as well as the ability to proceed sensitively without falling into the trap of heavy-handed state supervision. If in doubt, the course to follow will be self-regulation and relying on the power of the free market to correct its own abuses.

5. It took time to rein-in the mighty Robber Barons of the Gilded Age at the end of the 19th century, so the race we face will be a marathon and not a sprint. Forcing the modern Robber Barons to abandon their pernicious ways and behave responsibly will be a long haul, and regulation is only part of the solution. So, politicians, please proceed

with caution and finesse, with only as much regulation as necessary and as little as possible. Most importantly, in the immortal words of Bob Dylan: Your old road is rapidly aging. Please get out of the new one if you can't lend your hand – for the times they are a-changin'.

6. Just as the Sherman Antitrust Act took years before it was seriously applied to bust the trusts, we need to reckon with a long delay before the necessary measures adopted today, or in the near future, will lead to lasting effects on data monopolies and data misuse by the big tech companies and thus to lasting change. All the more important for us to take steps now!

7. Everyone has to do two things: die and pay taxes! That is, unless you're an internet behemoth like Amazon or Apple, then you can construct complicated tax shelters abroad and park your money there to avoid paying your dues back home. These companies have stashed away billions which could have been used to create jobs, repair America's crumbling infrastructure, provide universal healthcare and, in short, patch up the rifts in American society that are so very apparent in its present polarized society. We must end the practice of only taxing tech companies locally; instead, they must be forced to pay their fair share to the societies around the world in which they do business and reap gross levels of profits.

8. And while we're about it: What about the owners of the data these companies use to

grow fat at our expense? In a certain sense, we all work for Google, Amazon, Facebook and Apple by contributing details and highly personal information about ourselves for them to monetize. So why don't we have a say, a kind of digital workers' council. And why don't we get our just reward at the end of the year, like an employee payout. Of course, Big Tech won't volunteer to do this, so we need to put on pressure. The best way to achieve leverage would be solidarity! Why don't we all join together and create user unions at Google, Facebook and the others?

9. What if they refuse? Then maybe we will eventually have to take to the streets to demand our rights. Mass demonstrations work, as the example of those against the ACTA, SOPA and PIPA proved back in 2012 when the internet 'went on strike' and all three copyright infringement Acts, attempting to impose censorship through obsolete ideas about copyright, were derailed by public protests. We netizens are more powerful than we think – and we will need to flex our muscles when the time comes.

10. This struggle must result in a rethinking of our social norms and values. "Greed is cool" is not the slogan we need to create growth and prosperity for all. Our forefathers in the Gilded Age fought for social and economic justice and managed to drag the Robber Barons kicking and screaming into the Progressive Era and the Age of Reason along with their cronies in politics and government. And, like them, we need to persuade and, if necessary, force GAFA & Co to help us create

an age of justice and humanity. Yes, this sounds starry-eyed and society seems to be drifting in the opposite direction right now, if anything, but that is what it must have seemed like to folks back in the days of the Wild West, too. They have a lot to tell us. We should listen!

This short list is by no means exhaustive; quite the opposite. All of us – you, too, gentle reader – are called upon to play our part in determining where we want the road to the digital future to lead us.

So finally, this book – which was lots of fun to write – leaves me in a more pensive mood than before I started. The job we face is daunting, but it is also doable. All we need do is to follow the advice of one of the greatest minds of the European Enlightenment, Immanuel Kant:

"Sapere aude – dare to think for yourself!"

Bibliography

Gromball, Paul; Cole, Tim: *The Customer Cartel and the new power oft he customer in the Age of the Internet*, Hanser, 2000.

Hobbes, Thomas: *Leviathan*, 1986

Howe, Daniel Walker: *What Hath God Wrought – the Transformation of America*, Oxford University Press, 2009.

Leonhard, Gerd: *Technology vs. Humanity: Unsere Zukunft zwischen Mensch und Maschine*, Vahlen, 2018.

Loh, Janina: *Trans- and Posthumanity*, Junius, 2018.

Markoff, John: *Machines of Loving Grace: The Quest for Common Ground Between Humans and Robots*, Ecco, 2016.

Rifkin, Jeremy: *The Zero Marginal Cost Society: The Internet of Things, the Collaborative Commons, and the Eclipse of Capitalism*, Griffin, 2015.

Schrader, Matthias: *Transformational Products*, Next Factory Ottensen, 2018-.

Smith, Adam: *The Wealth of Nations*, W. Strahan and T. Cadell, 1776

Taplin, Jonathan: *Move Fast and Break Things: How Facebook, Google, and Amazon Cornered Culture and Undermined Democracy*, Pan, 2018.

Urchs, Ossi; Cole, Tim: *Digitale Enlightenment Now!*, Forsthaus, 2014.

Weigend, Andreas: *Data for the People: How to Make Our Post-Privacy Economy Work for You*, Basic Books, 2017.

Index